WHEN ARE WE EVER GONNA HAVE TO USE <u>THIS</u> ?

Updated Third Edition

HAL SAUNDERS

DALE SEYMOUR PUBLICATIONS®

Hal Saunders is a mathematics teacher at Dos Pueblos High School in the Santa Barbara School District. He has also co-authored with Robert A Carman the following texts:

Mathematics for the Trades: A Guided Approach (John Wiley and Sons, 1981, 1986)

Modern Technical Mathematics (Wadsworth, 1985)

Modern Technical Mathematics with Calculus (Wadsworth, 1985)

Illustrations by Jill Marino

Cover design and art by Bill Eral

Poster/chart design by Marin Graphics, Santa Barbara

Copyright © 1988 by Hal Saunders. Certain portions of this publication copyright 1981, 1980 by Hal Saunders. Published by Dale Seymour Publications®, an imprint of Pearson Learning Group, 299 Jefferson Road, Parsippany, NJ 07054. All rights reserved. No part of this book may be reproduced or transmitted in any form or by any means, electronic or mechanical, including photocopying, recording, or by any information storage and retrieval system, without permission in writing from the publisher, except for the problems, which may be reproduced for classroom use only.

ISBN 1-57232-364-7
Printed in the United States of America
17 18 19 20 21   06 05 04 03 02

1-800-321-3106
www.pearsonlearning.com

Contents

When Are We Ever Gonna Have to Use <u>This</u>?   iv
  Chart showing usage of mathematics
  in 100 occupations

Acknowledgments   vi

Preface   vii

Part 1: General Arithmetic
When Are We Ever Gonna Have to Use –
  Fractions   1
  Decimals   9
  Averages   19
  Ratio and Proportion   25
  Percent   35
  Statistical Graphing   53
  Miscellaneous Other Topics   62
    (Quick Computation, Rounding, Number Bases
    Other Than Ten, Scientific Notation, Probability,
    Negative Numbers)

Part 2: Practical Geometry
When Are We Ever Gonna Have to Use –
  Measurement and Conversion   68
  Area and Perimeter   75
  Volume   87
  The Pythagorean Theorem   93

Part 3: Elementary Algebra
When Are We Ever Gonna Have to Use –
  Formulas   96
  Linear Equations   117

Index to Occupations   125

Answers   129

Bibliography   133

Basic Math / Pre Algebra

Career columns (left to right):
Accountant (C.P.A.) · Advertising Account Exec. · Airline Flight Attendant · Airline Pilot (Commercial) · Architect · Assembler (Electronics) · Attorney · Auto Body Repair Worker · Auto Mechanic · Bank Teller · Biologist · Business Planner · Cable Splicer · Cameraperson (TV) · Carpenter · Ceramic Artist · Chef/Caterer · Chief Exec. Officer (Bank) · Chief Financial Officer (Bank) · Chiropractor · Computer Operator · Comp. Programmer (Business) · Computer Systems Analyst · Computer Technician (Micros) · Cosmetologist · Curator (Art Museum) · Dental Assistant · Dentist (General) · Dietitian · Disc Jockey · Disease Registry Technician · Doctor (Internist) · Drafter (Engineering) · Electrician (Engineering) · Electronics Technician (Residential) · (Aerospace) Engineer · (Air Quality) Engineer · (Chemical) Engineer · (Electronics) Engineer · (Mechanical) Engineer · (Microwave) Engineer · (Process) Engineer · (Quality Control) Engineer · (Structural) Engineer · Engineering Technician · Farm Operator · Financial Planner (Personal) · Firefighter · Forest Ecologist

Basic Math / Pre Algebra topics:
- Fractions
- Decimals
- Ratio and Proportion
- Percent
- Customary Measurement
- Metric Measurement
- Measurement Conversion
- Basic Probability
- Basic Statistics
- Statistical Graphing
- Powers and Roots
- Other Number Bases
- Negative Numbers
- Scientific Notation
- Basic Problem Solving

First-Year Algebra
- Using Formulas
- Linear Equations
- Linear Inequalities
- Operations w/ Polynomials
- Factoring Polynomials
- Rational Expressions
- Coordinate Graphing (2–D)
- Linear Systems
- Radicals
- Quadratic Equations
- Algebraic Representation

Geometry
- Basic Terminology
- Angle Measurement
- Congruent Triangles
- Triangle Inequalities
- Parallel Lines
- Quadrilaterals
- Similarity
- Geometric Mean
- Pythagorean Theorem
- Right Triangle Trig.
- Circles
- Constructions
- Area
- Volume
- Transformations
- Make/Use 3–D Drawings

Second-Year Algebra / Trigonometry
- Functions
- Variation
- Imaginary Numbers
- Polynomial Equations
- Logarithms
- Sequences and Series
- Matrices
- Coordinate Graphing (3–D)
- Advanced Probability
- Advanced Statistics
- Conic Sections
- Non-Linear Systems
- Trig./Circular Functions
- Graphs of Trig. Functions
- Trig. Identities
- Trig. Equations/Inverses
- Oblique Triangles
- Polar Coordinates/ Graphs
- Vectors

Other Topics
- Calculus and Higher Math
- Basic Calculator Use
- Scientific Calculator Use
- Computer Use
- Computer Programming
- Group Problem Solving
- Mental Math
- Induct./Deduct. Reasoning
- Math Communication
- Mathematical Modeling

This chart is available as a 34" x 22" poster from Dale Seymour Publications

Topic	Forestry Technician	General Contractor	Golf Pro	Graphic Artist	Highway Patrol Officer	Homemaker	Instrument Tech. (Air Quality)	Insurance Agent	Interior Designer	International Marketer	Landscape Gardener	Librarian (Cataloguing)	Machinist (Prototype)	Market Researcher	Medical Lab Technologist	Medical Researcher	Motel Manager	Newspaper Reporter	Nuclear Medicine Tech.	Nurse	Optician	Optometrist	Painting Contractor	Paralegal	Payroll Supervisor	Personnel Manager	Pharmacist (Community)	Photographer (Commercial)	Physical Therapist	Physicist (Research)	Plumber	Printer	Psychotherapist	Public Relations Director	Real Estate Agent	Recreation Supervisor	Restaurant Manager	Retail Salesperson	Road Maintenance Worker	Secretary (Administrative)	Small Business Owner	Stock Broker	Surveyor (Land)	Travel Agent	Urban Planner	Veterinarian	Wage / Salary Analyst	Waiter / Waitress	Welder - Fabricator	X-Ray Technician
Basic Math / Pre Algebra																																																		
Fractions	●	●		●		●	●		●	●	●	●	●	●	●	●		●	●	●	●	●	●	●	●	●	●	●		●	●	●		●	●					●	●	●		●	●	●	●	●	●	●
Decimals	●	●	●	●	●	●	●	●	●	●	●	●	●	●	●	●	●	●	●	●	●	●	●	●	●	●	●	●	●	●	●	●	●	●	●	●	●	●	●	●	●	●	●	●	●	●	●	●	●	●
Ratio and Proportion	●	●	●	●		●	●	●		●	●	●	●	●	●	●		●	●	●	●	●	●			●	●	●	●	●	●	●	●	●	●	●	●				●	●	●		●	●	●		●	
Percent	●	●	●	●	●	●	●	●	●	●	●	●	●	●	●	●	●	●		●	●	●	●	●	●	●	●		●	●	●	●	●	●	●	●	●	●	●	●	●	●	●	●	●	●	●	●		●
Customary Measurement	●	●	●	●	●	●	●	●	●	●	●	●	●		●	●	●	●	●	●	●	●	●			●	●	●	●	●	●	●	●	●	●	●	●	●	●		●	●	●	●	●	●	●		●	●
Metric Measurement		●		●	●	●	●			●					●	●		●	●	●	●	●					●	●	●	●	●						●		●		●	●	●	●		●	●			●
Measurement Conversion	●	●	●	●	●	●	●		●	●	●		●		●	●		●	●	●	●	●	●			●	●	●	●	●	●	●		●	●			●	●		●	●	●	●	●	●			●	●
Basic Probability		●	●									●		●		●		●	●	●		●							●	●		●		●		●						●	●		●	●				●
Basic Statistics	●	●	●	●	●	●	●		●	●		●		●	●	●	●	●	●	●	●	●	●			●	●		●	●		●	●	●	●	●	●		●		●	●	●	●	●	●	●			
Statistical Graphing	●	●	●			●	●	●	●	●	●	●		●	●	●		●	●	●	●	●	●			●	●	●	●	●			●	●	●	●	●				●	●		●	●	●	●			
Powers and Roots	●	●			●		●				●		●	●	●	●			●		●							●	●	●							●						●		●	●	●		●	●
Other Number Bases							●						●		●															●																				
Negative Numbers	●		●		●	●	●	●				●	●	●	●	●		●	●	●	●	●		●		●	●	●		●				●	●	●	●				●	●	●		●	●	●			
Scientific Notation							●						●	●	●	●			●			●								●																●				
Basic Problem Solving	●	●	●	●	●	●	●	●	●	●	●	●	●	●	●	●	●	●	●	●	●	●	●	●	●	●	●	●	●	●	●	●	●	●	●	●	●	●	●		●	●	●	●	●	●	●		●	●
First-Year Algebra																																																		
Using Formulas	●	●	●	●	●	●	●	●	●		●		●	●	●	●	●	●	●	●	●	●	●	●	●	●	●	●	●	●	●	●	●		●		●		●		●	●	●	●	●	●	●		●	●
Linear Equations	●	●					●					●	●	●	●	●			●	●		●		●		●	●		●	●		●									●	●	●		●	●	●			
Linear Inequalities														●		●														●															●					
Operations w/ Polynomials																●														●																				
Factoring Polynomials																●														●																				
Rational Expressions																●														●																				
Coordinate Graphing (2–D)							●					●		●	●	●						●								●												●	●		●		●			
Linear Systems														●		●														●															●		●			
Radicals																														●																				
Quadratic Equations																●														●																	●			
Algebraic Representation							●							●	●	●			●			●		●						●											●	●	●		●	●	●			
Geometry																																																		
Basic Terminology	●	●	●	●	●	●	●	●	●		●		●	●	●	●		●	●	●	●	●	●						●	●	●	●		●	●	●	●		●		●		●	●	●	●			●	●
Angle Measurement	●	●	●	●	●	●	●		●		●	●	●		●	●		●	●	●	●	●		●				●	●	●	●	●					●	●				●		●		●	●			●	●
Congruent Triangles		●																												●													●							
Triangle Inequalities		●	●																											●													●							
Parallel Lines		●	●										●	●									●							●													●			●				
Quadrilaterals	●	●					●						●																	●													●						●	
Similarity	●	●		●									●			●		●	●			●						●		●		●											●							
Geometric Mean							●							●		●			●			●								●																	●			
Pythagorean Theorem	●	●					●				●		●								●	●								●													●			●			●	
Right Triangle Trig.							●						●			●						●								●													●		●					
Circles		●	●		●								●	●		●						●								●													●			●				
Constructions							●						●	●															●	●													●							
Area	●	●				●	●	●	●	●	●	●	●	●		●	●	●	●			●	●			●		●		●	●	●		●	●	●	●		●		●		●		●	●			●	
Volume	●	●					●			●	●	●	●	●		●		●				●				●				●	●	●						●		●		●		●		●	●			●	
Transformations				●									●	●									●								●													●							
Make/Use 3–D Drawings	●	●	●	●			●		●		●		●	●	●	●			●		●	●						●	●	●	●				●				●		●		●		●	●			●	●
Second-Year Algebra / Trigonometry																																																		
Functions							●							●		●						●								●																				
Variation							●							●		●			●									●		●												●				●				●
Imaginary Numbers																														●																				
Polynomial Equations																														●																				
Logarithms							●							●		●			●			●								●																				
Sequences and Series																														●																	●			
Matrices														●																●																				
Coordinate Graphing (3–D)														●																●																				
Advanced Probability														●		●														●																				
Advanced Statistics							●							●	●	●			●			●					●			●													●				●			
Conic Sections													●			●														●																				
Non-Linear Systems																●														●																				
Trig./Circular Functions													●			●														●													●							
Graphs of Trig. Functions																●														●																				
Trig. Identities																														●																				
Trig. Equations/Inverses																														●																				
Oblique Triangles													●																	●													●							
Polar Coordinates/ Graphs													●																	●													●							
Vectors							●						●	●		●														●																				
Other Topics																																																		
Calculus and Higher Math																														●																				
Basic Calculator Use	●	●	●	●		●	●	●	●	●	●	●	●	●	●	●	●	●	●	●	●		●	●	●	●	●	●	●	●		●		●	●	●	●	●		●	●	●	●	●	●	●	●	●	●	●
Scientific Calculator Use							●						●	●	●	●														●													●							
Computer Use	●	●	●	●	●	●	●	●	●	●		●	●	●	●	●	●	●	●	●			●	●	●	●	●	●	●	●		●	●	●	●	●	●			●	●	●	●	●	●	●	●			●
Computer Programming													●	●																●																	●			
Group Problem Solving	●	●	●	●	●	●	●	●	●	●		●	●	●	●	●	●	●	●	●	●	●	●	●	●	●		●	●	●	●	●	●	●	●	●	●	●	●		●	●	●	●	●	●	●			●
Mental Math	●	●	●	●	●	●	●	●	●	●	●	●	●	●	●	●		●	●	●	●	●	●	●		●	●	●	●	●	●	●	●	●	●	●		●	●	●	●	●	●	●	●	●	●	●	●	●
Induct./Deduct. Reasoning	●	●	●	●			●	●	●	●	●	●	●	●	●	●		●		●		●		●		●		●	●	●	●	●	●	●		●					●	●	●	●	●	●	●			
Math Communication		●	●				●						●	●		●						●							●	●			●													●	●			●
Mathematical Modeling														●		●			●			●								●											●		●		●		●			

3rd edition, © 1991 by Hal Saunders

Acknowledgments

The following friends and colleagues were of great help and assistance to me in writing and publishing this book:

Helen Barron, Bob Carman, Laurie Carman, Lyn Carman, Mike Champe, Wayne Cole, Marlinde Jurgensen, Linda Lyon, Rick Mokler, Steve Rainen and Peter Walsh at the Computer Shop, and my wife Chrissy, who was particularly helpful in doing research for this revised third edition

The following people either submitted or gave ideas for the problems:

Tracy Abels, Richard Achey, Gloria Acunia, Sam Alfano, Bob Alvord, M. E. Appel, Edward Arbuckle, Ugo Arnoldi, Steve Backland, Lee Banson, M. Scott Barnes, Brian Barnwell, Steve Bartnicki, Chief Kenneth Bishop, Jack L. Bivins, Robert Blau, Bob Blecker, James Bradsberry, Jim Brown, Sgt. Quentin Brown, Lars Bruun-Anderson, Karyle Butcher, Yvonne Chan, Jim Chesher, Captain William Christiansen, Marjorie Clark, Stephen Clark, Larry Cochran, John Coleman, Joseph Connell, Steve Cooley, Harold Cooper, Pat Damron, Bonnie De Simone, Harry Dickinson, Michael Dockery, George Dumas, Dennis Ensign, Anna Estrada, John Evans, Howard Feinstein, Marjorie Finkelson, Larry Finley, Bryon Forbes, L. R. Ford, Dennis Frederick, Doug Geneau, Tom Giordano, Officer Kenneth Gouff, Roger Grigsby, Art Grossman, Dave Haggard, Bill Hamilton, Bill Hanna, Walter Hausz, Howard Hawthorne, Derek Hedges, Bill Heidler, Robert Holmes, Mike Hopkins, Larry Hornberger, Dougal House, Phyllis Ingers, Peter Jackson, W. H. Jago, Carl Jeffries, Steve Jones, Clifford Jourdan, Chuck Kelsey, Dr. Ronald Kemp, Robert L. Kingery, Art Kluge, J. C. Lansing, John Lippis, Gerald Little, Shelly Lowenkopf, Lynn Lown, Norman H. Macleod, Alan Manet, Rex Marchbanks, Anthony Marino, Jill Marino, Peggy Martin, Serge Matlovsky, Janet McCann, Al McCurdy, Pete McGowan, John McKee, Jim McKinney, Ralph McNall, John Merritt, John J. Michael, Barbara Mokler, Bernard E. Monahan, Baker Moore, Don Morrison, Brad Nagle, Bernard Parent, William Pence, Jamie Pfeiffer, Jim Pollock, Mike Pyzell, Robert Rankin, Emil Richter, Clark Ritchie, R. A. Ritchie, Ralph Remick, Fred Rice, David Rood, Elliot Rosenblum, Betty Rosness, Galen Sandwisch, Lee Schaller, James Selover, Ken Shamordola, Gary Shaw, Cliff Sprague, Claus Stapleman, George Stockton, Gary Stoll, Joann Sullins, Dan Sullivan, William Sykes, George Taylor, Steve Turnbull, Dennis Wagner, Jim Wahl, Dave Waite, Dan Waltmann, Dr. Alan A. Wilcox, Julie Wood, Jim Wootton, Jim Wright, Morris Zimmerman

In addition to these people, I would like to thank the many others who consented to interviews to verify the information contained in the charts on pages iv and v.

Preface

As math teachers, we feel certain that most of what we teach has practical value. However, since the majority of us have little or no experience in other areas, we are not familiar with the various applications of our material. Some of the textbooks we rely on do not help much when they pose such problems as:

> "Joe sat on his front lawn counting cars. Of the first 30 passing by, 12 were black. What percent were black?"

"Who cares?" would be the reply of a typical junior high student.

Then there are those that only seem to have practical value:

> "A 12-foot ladder is leaned up against a building. How far from the base of the building must the foot of the ladder be in order to reach a window 9 feet high?"

How many people would really go to the trouble of using the Pythagorean theorem when they can just lean the ladder up against the wall and see the distance for themselves?

Since I was not always able to answer the question, "When are we ever gonna have to use this?" I decided to venture into the outside world and seek the answers. I interviewed people representing 100 different occupations to find out which of some 60 math topics they used, and how they used them. As a result of the interviews, I was able to construct the charts on pages iv and v and formulate the 435 word problems that make up the remainder of the book.

Using the Problems

Teachers and students can use the word problems in two ways. If you are studying a particular math concept and wonder how people use it in the real world, refer to the chapter dealing with that topic. If you or your students are curious about how people use math in a specific occupation, consult the index on pages 125–127 for a list of problems dealing with that occupation.

The problems within each chapter are arranged alphabetically according to occupation, not according to complexity. However, after each occupational title is a Roman numeral indicating the difficulty level of the problem (I—easy; II—medium; III—challenging). Many problems include explanations of how they arise, and the more complex problems are preceded by worked examples or hints. Since realistic numbers are used, the aid of a calculator is recommended for the more difficult problems.

Almost all the problems were taken from direct interviews and questionnaires. However, some of the people referred to various training manuals and code books when asked for illustrations of typical on-the-job problems. These sources are identified in a bibliography on page 133. A few of the problems (noted with *) were excerpted from *Mathematics for the Trades: A Guided Approach* by Robert A. Carman and Hal M. Saunders (John Wiley and Sons, New York, 1981). We used similar research techniques in gathering material for this book.

In this revised third edition of *When Are We Ever Gonna Have to Use This?* many of the original problems have been updated or replaced to reflect current prices and costs, as well as new laws and procedures. Furthermore, two new sections of elementary algebra (formulas and linear equations) have been included, and several new problems have been added to the original sections.

Using the Charts

Because each and every application of math listed could not be illustrated by a word problem, the charts on pages iv and v are intended to show all the math topics used by each of the 100 different occupations. The charts have the same cross-referencing feature as the problems. You can either find all the occupations that use a particular math concept or all the math concepts used by a particular occupation.

The purpose of the charts is to show which math concepts are actually applied by people in their work. In some areas, most notably health fields (doctors, dentists, etc.), the math required to qualify for the occupation goes beyond what is actually performed on the job. This is usually done to provide people with both an understanding of the concepts behind the applications and the tools to do research in their field.

Although the charts provide an accurate picture for those interviewed, it should be noted that not everyone in the same occupation uses the same amount of math. Some people specialize in different aspects of the job than others. Variations in math usage can also be attributed to differences in individual math backgrounds. Those who go further in math tend to apply more math and do their jobs with added efficiency because of it. For example, attorneys with strong math backgrounds can handle more technical cases. Sheet metal workers who can do trigonometry are in much greater demand than those who cannot. A business manager who takes algebra can develop formulas that save time and money. In general, what math teachers have been preaching for years has been proven once again with an added wrinkle: Not only do you qualify for more jobs with a stronger math background, but you can also perform many jobs with added success.

With organizations such as the NCTM encouraging the use of relevant word problems in the curriculum of the '80s and '90s, I hope that this publication will be a useful source of such problems. I also hope it will help you answer the question: "When are we ever gonna have to use *this*?"

Hal M. Saunders
Santa Barbara, California

Part 1: General Arithmetic

When Are We Ever Gonna Have to Use — Fractions?

1. **Advertising Agent** (I)

   An agent has placed newspaper ads of 6 1/2 c.i. (column inches), 5 3/4 c.i., 3 1/4 c.i., 4 3/4 c.i., and 5 c.i. At the rate of $16 per column inch, find the total cost of the ads.

2. **Airplane Mechanic** (I)

   The "aileron droop" of a certain plane must be adjusted to 7/8 inch plus or minus 1/4 inch. Given this leeway (called "tolerance"), what is the maximum droop allowed?

3. **Airplane Mechanic** (II)

   A piece of tubing 9 5/8 inches long is cut from a piece 33 1/2 inches long. Allowing 1/16 inch for the cut, how much is left?

4. **Airplane Mechanic** (III)

   Drill sizes are in fractions, yet many dimensions are often given as decimals. A blueprint calls for a hole of 0.391 inch. Find the fractional drill size required if the hole must be drilled 1/64 inch smaller than the size of the hole called for in the blueprint. (**Hint:** Convert the decimal size to a fraction with a denominator of 64. Round to the nearest 64th.)

5. **Airplane Pilot** (I)

   A plane is consuming fuel at the rate of 7 1/2 gallons per hour. The pilot has 18 gallons remaining. How long will the fuel last?

6. **Architect * (also Drafter)** (I)

   If 1/4 inch represents 1 foot on a blueprint, how many inches on the drawing will be required to represent 18 feet?

7. **Attorney** (III)

   The Justice Department is suing Sage Brush Independent School District to obtain special education facilities for handicapped children. As the attorney on the case, you must first show the court the total budget for the coming school year.

State aid to the district will be $105 per average daily attendance. In addition, local funds will be increased by 7/12 of the total local budget through additional property taxes.

Average daily attendance is projected at 35,185; total local budget will be $2,150,000; federal funds amount to $35,000,000. Find the amount of state aid, the extra amount of local funds, and the total budget for Sage Brush.

8. **Auto Mechanic** (II)

A bearing, measured at 1.234 inches with a caliper, must be replaced. Since the bearings are sized in 64ths of an inch, find the closest fractional size.

9. **Carpenter** (II)

A two-by-four has a finished width of about 3 1/2 inches. How many two-by-fours are needed to complete a deck 26 feet 8 inches wide? (Assume no spacing between the boards.)

10. **Carpenter *** (I)

A 2 1/4-inch nail is driven through a board 1 3/8 inches thick supporting a joist. How far into the joist does the nail extend?

11. **Computer Systems Engineer** (II)

While explaining the advantages of purchasing a computer to a potential customer, a systems engineer will point out the tax advantage of depreciating the value of the computer over a period of time. Using the straight-line method of depreciation, suppose that a $10,000 computer with a salvage value of $1000 is depreciated over a 5-year period. The tax depreciation claimed per year would be 1/5 of $9000 (the difference between cost and salvage value), or $1800.

Find the yearly depreciation of a $16,000 computer with a $1500 salvage value if it is depreciated over a 5-year period.

12. **Dietician** (I)

A hospitalized diabetic is on a carefully controlled 2000-calorie diet distributed over five feedings per day. There are two heavy feedings consisting of 2/7 of the total calories each. There are also

When Are We Ever Gonna Have to Use This?

three light feedings consisting of 1/7 of the total each. Determine the number of calories for a heavy feeding and for a light feeding.

13. **Drafter** (III)

A cabinet 30 inches high must have a 4-inch thick base and a 1 1/2-inch thick top. Four equal-sized drawers must fit in the remaining space, with 3/4 inch between drawers. What is the height of each drawer?

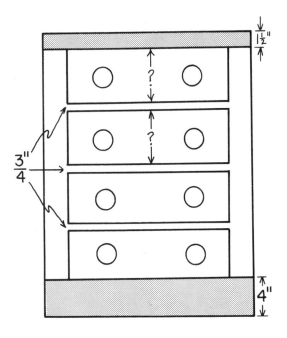

14. **Drafter** (III)

A cabinet 10 feet long must have 5 doors. There are 1 1/2-inch wide stiles between the doors and at both ends. What is the width of each door? (Round to the nearest 16th of an inch.)

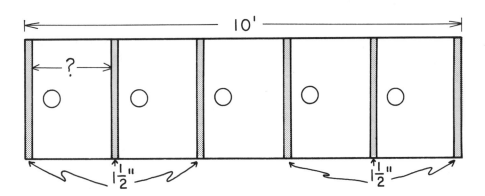

15. **Electrician * (I)**

What would be the output voltage on a 115-volt line with a voltage drop of 6 3/4 volts from panel bus to outlet?

16. **Flooring Contractor * (II)**

How many boards 4 5/8 inches wide will it take to cover a floor 18 1/2 feet wide?

17. **Income Tax Specialist (I)**

A client and his wife jointly own 2/5 of a house in partnership with others. During the tax year the home was sold for a gain of $25,400. What amount of gain is reportable for the couple?

18. **Income Tax Specialist (II)**

The total interest on a 3-year business loan is $150. The borrower had the loan for 8 months of the tax year.

a. What fraction of the interest is deductible for the year?

b. How much does this amount to?

19. **Insurance Claims Supervisor (II)**

Insurance claims are usually paid based on the depreciated value of the item in question. An item stolen or destroyed with half its useful life remaining would bring a payment equal to half its original cost. If a battery was stolen when it was 5 months old, find the depreciated value if the battery cost $45 new and was guaranteed for 36 months.

20. **Interior Decorator (I)**

A customer wants a fireplace front 3 inches thick made of a synthetic material called Corian. If Corian comes in 3/4-inch thick sheets, how many sheets must be ordered?

21. **Masonry Contractor * (II)**

If we allow 2 5/8 inches for the height of a row of bricks (including mortar), how many rows will be needed for a wall 3 feet 11 1/4 inches high?

22. **Medical Lab Technician** (II)

In order to determine the potency of a certain disease in a sample of blood, a medical lab technician must find the smallest concentration of blood that reacts with a serum. The technician performs a serial dilution in which she first takes 1/2 milliliter of blood and mixes it with 1/2 milliliter of water, then takes 1/2 milliliter of this first dilution and again mixes it with 1/2 milliliter of water to obtain a second dilution, and so on. She continues to dilute the blood in this manner and finds that the blood in the tenth dilution is the last one that reacts with the serum. Express the concentration of blood in the tenth dilution as a fraction.

23. **Newspaper Production Worker** * (I)

A photograph must be reduced to 4/5 of its original size to fit the space available in a newspaper. Find the length of the reduced photograph if the original was 6 3/4 inches long.

24. **Nurse** (III)

The doctor prescribes a 1000-cc intravenous bottle to be given to a patient over an 8-hour period. The nurse must set the drip rate of the bottle. Find the number of drops per minute if there are 15 drops per cc.

25. **Nurse** (I)

The doctor prescribes 25 grains of a medicine that comes only in 10-grain tablets. How many tablets do you give the patient?

26. **Nurse** (III)

The doctor orders 20 grains of a medicine that comes only in 500-mg tablets. If 500 mg equals 8 1/3 grains, how many tablets do you give the patient?

27. **Nurse** (II)

A doctor orders 1/400 of a grain of medication. The nurse has a vial labeled 1/200 grains per cc (cubic centimeter). How many cc does the nurse give the patient?

28. Photographer (III)

An 8" by 10" photograph must be mounted on an 11" by 14" mat subject to the following conditions:

1. There should be an extra 1/4" margin on all four sides of the hole cut for the photograph.

2. The photograph must be centered horizontally.

3. The photograph must be mounted one inch above the vertical center of the mat.

Find the margins on all four sides of the mat.

29. Plumber * (I)

While installing water pipes, a plumber used pieces of pipe measuring 2 3/4 feet, 4 1/3 feet, 3 1/2 feet, and 1 1/4 feet. How much pipe would remain if these pieces were cut from a 14-foot length of pipe? (Ignore waste in cutting.)

30. Plumber (County Inspector) (I)

Slope measurements in inches of rise or fall per foot are important because slope is regulated by the building code. If the full length of a house sewer is 120 feet, and the total fall is 30 inches, what is the slope?

31. Political Campaign Manager (I)

Before ordering campaign literature for a mailing, the campaign manager needs to know how many households there are among all registered voters. The rule of thumb is that there are 2/3 as many households as there are registered voters. How many copies of a mailer should be ordered for a district in which there are 148,500 registered voters?

32. Printer (I)

Your warehouse supervisor reports a total of 1 1/2 rolls of a certain kind of paper. You have three jobs that utilize this paper today. One job requires 1/4 roll, another requires 2/5 roll, and the third needs 1/2 roll. Are you overstocked or understocked for the jobs? By how much?

33. Publishing House Production Manager (II)

The pages for a book are to be 6" wide. If the type being used is 1/6" per character, how much of the page width is left for margins with a 26-character line?

34. Real Estate Agent (II)

If a person is selling the north half of the northwest quarter of an 880-acre piece of land, how many acres will be left?

35. Social Worker (III)

A mother with two children is entitled to a maximum welfare grant of $633 per month. If she works, however, part of her earnings are applied to this amount. To determine the actual grant of a working mother, follow this procedure:

1. Subtract $75 from her monthly earnings for work-related expenses.

2. Subtract child-care expenses of up to $160 per child.

3. Subtract $30 per month.

4. Subtract 1/3 of what remains.

5. Subtract this amount from $633.

Determine the total grant for a mother with two children, who earns $600 per month, and whose child-care expenses amount to $100 per month per child.

36. Stockbroker (II)

Three hundred shares of stock are purchased at $37 1/2 per share and sold at $49 1/8 per share. What is the gross profit?

37. Title Insurance Officer (I)

The annual property tax on a home just sold is $1548. If the seller lived there for four months of the year before the sale, how much of the tax is owed on a pro-rata basis?

38.   **Travel Agent** (II)

Normal round trip fare to Europe is $864. If children can fly for 2/3 fare, determine the total round trip fare for a family of two adults and four children.

39.   **Welder *** (I)

In a particular welding job, three pieces of I-beam with lengths of 5 7/8 inches, 8 1/2 inches, and 22 3/4 inches are needed. What is the total length of I-beam needed?

When Are We Ever Gonna Have to Use — Decimals?

1. **Airplane Mechanic** (I)

   The "mean chord" of the wings of an airplane is equal to its wing area divided by its wing span. Find the mean chord of a plane if its wing area is 275 square feet and its span is 42.25 feet. (Round to the nearest hundredth.)

2. **Airplane Pilot (also Airplane Mechanic)** (III)

   The pilot of a small airplane is responsible for loading the aircraft so that the center of gravity is within certain safe limits. This ensures that the plane will fly safely, especially in case of engine failure.

   To find the center of gravity, the pilot multiplies the weight of everything on the plane by its arm or distance from a certain point called the "datum." This product is called the "moment" of each weight. The sum of the moments, divided by the total weight of all the objects, equals the distance of the center of gravity from the datum. The pilot then checks this result with a graph or chart to see if it is within safe limits. If it is not, the pilot must re-balance the weight.

   The chart that follows shows the information necessary to find the center of gravity of a particular airplane. For each location, multiply the weight by the arm (distance) to find the moment. Then add the moments, divide this by the total weight, and round to the nearest tenth. See if this center of gravity is under 82.1, the safe limit for this plane.

Location	Weight	Arm
Empty weight	2181 lb	80 in.
Front seats	340	85
Rear seats	125	117
Oil	30	−24
Fuel	444	75

   Note: Since the arm distance for oil is negative, you must subtract its moment from the total instead of adding it.

3. **Appliance Store Manager** (I)

To calculate the number of BTU necessary for a customer's air conditioning system, multiply the area of the room by the "exposure factor" and then by the "climate factor." Find the number of BTU for an air conditioning system in a 640-square-foot room with a south exposure (exposure factor of 30) in Seattle (climate factor of 0.95).

4. **Appraiser (Real Estate)** (II)

In a certain neighborhood, houses are valued at $50 per square foot, patios at $2.50 per square foot, driveways at $0.95 per square foot, and fences at $6.75 per linear foot. Determine the value of a 1950-square-foot house with 350 square feet of patio, 720 square feet of driveway, and 400 feet of fence.

5. **Architect** (I)

If a beam weighs 32 pounds per foot, what is the weight of a beam 4.8 feet long?

6. **Auto Mechanic** (III)

The valve clearance in an automobile's engine must be measured very precisely. If the clearance is not correct, a "shim" is put in place that takes up just enough room to make it correct.

For example, if the intake valve is supposed to have a 0.008-inch clearance, and the mechanic measures it to be 0.021 inches, he knows that he needs a shim that is 0.013 inches larger than the old one. If the old one was 0.089 inches, it must be replaced with a 0.102-inch shim.

Suppose the valve clearance for exhaust is supposed to be 0.017 inches. Right now it measures 0.009 inches. If the present shim measures 0.0115 inches, what size shim must it be replaced with to achieve the proper clearance?

7. **Carpenter** * (III)

Find the total bill for a job in which materials cost $678.12 and labor amounted to 16.5 hours at $32 per hour.

8. Carpenter (I)

Twelve equally spaced holes are to be drilled in a plywood strip
34 3/4 inches long. There must also be 2 inches from each end to
the center of the first hole on each end. To the nearest hundredth
of an inch, what is the distance from center to center of two
consecutive holes?

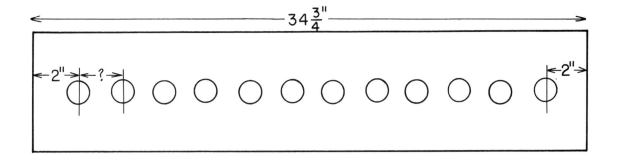

9. Carpet Cleaner (II)

Many carpet cleaners charge according to the area of the carpet,
often calculated to the nearest tenth of a square foot. They also
vary their price according to the difficulty of the particular carpet.

Determine the total cost of the following job:

Type of Carpet	Area (sq ft)	Cost per Sq Ft
Wall-to-wall short pile	418	$0.24
Wall-to-wall deep shag	268	0.30
Area rug on premises	177.4	0.40
Area rug at plant	209.8	0.75

10. Civil Engineer (III)

A civil engineer working for the County Building and Safety
Department must determine whether or not building plans
conform to code specifications. For example, the two supporting
side walls of a building are only allowed to bear a certain
maximum amount of weight per linear foot. To compute this, an
engineer would find the total weight per square foot of all roofing
materials, multiply by the number of square feet of roof surface,
and divide by the total number of linear feet in the two side walls.

Suppose plans are submitted for a 20-foot square garage. The 400
square feet of built-up roofing weighs 5.5 pounds per square foot.

The joists supporting the roofing weigh 1.54 pounds per square foot, and the 1/2-in. plywood between the joists and the roof weighs 1.5 pounds per square foot. How much weight will the 40 feet of side walls have to bear per linear foot?

11.   Controller (II)

Since payroll taxes are not applied to sick leave, the controller must calculate the total wages for sick leave separately from the wages for all other hours. If an employee had 119 total hours, including 5.5 hours of sick leave, calculate:

a. the sick leave wages

b. the wages for the remaining hours

The employee's pay rate is $6.2826 per hour. (Round to the nearest cent.)

12.   Electrician (II)

When running wires over a long distance, electricians must be concerned with voltage drop. If the drop in voltage amounts to 0.0339 volts per ampere per 100 feet, how much of a drop will there be for 20 amperes at 350 feet?

13.   Fire Fighter (I)

When calculating friction loss in a hose with a diameter other than 2.5 inches, a fire fighter first uses a formula or chart to determine friction loss in a 2.5-inch hose and then divides by a constant given in a table.

At 300 gallons per minute, the friction loss in 500 feet of 2.5-inch hose is 105 pounds. What would the friction loss be in 3.5-inch hose if the constant given in the table is 5.8?

14.   Highway Patrol Officer (II)

At the end of a working day, highway patrol officers must report the total amount of time spent performing certain types of tasks. During one 8-hour shift, an officer spent 45 minutes aiding vehicles in distress, 1 1/2 hours at the scene of an accident, and 2 hours 20 minutes writing tickets. To the nearest tenth of an hour, how much time was spent not performing these specific tasks?

15. **Interior Decorator** (III)

To calculate the total cost of a carpeting job, a decorator first finds the retail cost of all materials. But since tax can be charged only on the wholesale cost, the decorator must also compute this figure in order to find the tax. The reason is that the difference between retail and wholesale is labor, and tax is not applied to labor.

Determine the total cost of the following carpeting job: 60 square yards of carpet at $24.95 per square yard, 60 square yards of pad at $2.50 per square yard, and 96 feet of tackless strip at $0.75 per foot. Add to this 6% sales tax on the wholesale price of all materials: $18.50 per square yard for the carpet, $1.60 per square yard for the pad, and $0.35 per foot for the strip.

(**Hint:** Notice that you must really work two problems. First figure the total retail cost. Then calculate the wholesale cost of all materials in order to determine the sales tax. Just multiply the wholesale cost by 0.06 to compute the tax.)

16. **Machinist** * (I)

Each inch of 1-inch-diameter cold-rolled steel weighs 0.22 pound. How much does a 38-inch piece weigh?

17. **Masonry Contractor** (I)

The rule of thumb in brickwork is that there are 6.5 bricks per square foot. Estimate the total number of bricks needed for a 1250-square-foot wall.

18. **Medical Lab Technician** (I)

In determining the number of "eosinophils" (a type of white blood cell) per cubic millimeter, lab technicians first count the number of such cells in a specific area under a microscope and then multiply by an area factor of 5.5.

If there are 91 eosinophils in the designated area, what is the count per cubic millimeter?

19. **Medical Lab Technician** (I)

An examination of a parasite egg in a lab specimen shows it to be 8 units long in a microscopic field. If each unit is 2.3 microns long, how long is the egg (measured in microns) ?

20. Nurse (I)

The doctor orders 0.1 gram of nicotinic acid for a patient. If it is only available in 0.05-gram tablets, how many tablets do you give the patient?

21. Payroll Supervisor (II)

The payroll supervisor must compute the amount of withholding tax to deduct from every employee's check. An employee making $475.50 per week before taxes must pay $4450.68 withholding tax over the course of the year.

a. How much withholding tax must be paid per week?

b. What would the employee's weekly check be after deducting this tax?

22. Petroleum Engineer (I)

The minimum thickness for a spherical steel gas storage tank is 0.45 inch. However, in designing such a tank, officials multiply the minimum thickness by a factor of 2.5 for added safety. Find the "safe" thickness for the tank.

23. Plumber (County Inspector) (II)

In a percolation test on a seepage pit to be used for a septic tank, the percolation rate per hour was calculated to be 1.83 gallons per square foot. How much would this amount to in 24 hours for a 120-square-foot pit?

24. Plumber (County Inspector) (II)

Plumbing code dictates that a particular disposal field for a septic tank must absorb 5000 gallons per day. Percolation tests on the soil show a rate of absorption equal to 14.86 gallons per square foot per day. How many square feet must the trench bottom be in order to absorb the required amount? (Round to the nearest square foot.)

25. Police Officer (I)

The reserve corps contributed 7819 hours of duty at a value of $10.25 per hour last year. How much was this worth to the department?

26. **Political Campaign Manager** (II)

How much money do you need to send 120,000 pieces of regular-sized campaign literature at 16.7 cents per piece (bulk rate) and 7000 personal donation requests at 25 cents per piece?

27. **Printer** (III)

A customer orders a job requiring 2500 sheets of paper. The printer has a choice of ordering a full carton of 3000 sheets at $27.20 per thousand or "breaking" a carton (ordering exactly the number of sheets required) and paying $38.40 per thousand. Which would be less expensive in this case?

28. **Printer** (I)

The cost per thousand of running a job is $53.75. What is the cost for printing 5000 copies?

29. **Printer** (III)

A particular printing job requires the printer to shoot some negatives. One process called "single burn" requires 8 negatives at $12.38 each. This process also requires 2.8 units of labor (a unit is 10 minutes) at $60 per hour. The "double burn" process requires only 4 negatives at $12.38 each. However, this process requires 5.5 units of labor at $60 per hour. (Remember, a unit is 10 minutes.) Find the total cost of each process.

30. **Publishing House Production Manager** (III)

The production manager has a book with the following characteristics:

- It contains a total of 863,900 characters.

- It has a line length of 30 picas.

- It has a page length of 48 lines.

- It uses print that yields 2.6 characters per pica.

Calculate the total number of pages the book will run by following these steps:

a. Multiply the line length by the number of characters per pica. This gives you the number of characters per line.

b. Multiply the characters per line by the page length. This gives you the number of characters per page.

c. Divide the characters per page into the total number of characters in the book and round to the nearest whole number. This gives you the number of pages of text.

d. Round the number of pages of text up to the next multiple of 16. (The book is bound in 16-page sections.) This is the total number of pages the book will run.

Note: The next three problems illustrate the steps a publisher follows to determine the production cost of a book. After adding royalties and a certain percent of profit (see problem 57, page 48 in the section on percent), the publisher arrives at the selling price of the book.

31. Publishing House Production Manager (II)

To determine the unit price (price per copy) for typesetting a book, multiply the number of pages per book by the cost per page and divide by the number of copies to be printed.

Determine the unit price for typesetting a 240-page book at $15.45 per page if the publisher will print 1800 copies.

32. Publishing House Production Manager (II)

To determine the unit price for printing a book, divide the total cost of printing by the number of copies printed. Suppose a printer charges $8100 to print 1800 copies of a book. What is the unit cost of printing?

33. Publishing House Production Manager (II)

After finding the unit costs of typesetting and printing (see problems 31 and 32), the next step in determining the cost of a book is to calculate the unit cost of "in-house items"—production time and advertising.

The production manager spent 25 hours on the book at $25 per hour. The manager's assistant spent 19 hours on the book at $12.50 per hour.

a. Calculate the total cost of production time.

b. For 1800 copies, what would the unit cost of production time be?

c. If advertising costs $1.75 per copy, what is the total unit cost of the two "in-house" items?

34. **Real Estate Agent** (I)

A $7560 loan is paid off at the rate of $52.50 per month. How long will it take to pay off the loan?

35. **Savings and Loan Counselor** (I)

A customer deposits a check for 4500 francs. The daily exchange rate is $0.1680 per franc. How much is this in U.S. currency?

36. **Sheet Metal, Heating, and Air Conditioning Specialist** (III)

An important measurement in planning a solar heating system is the "coefficient of heat transfer." To compute this, first find the sum of the heat loss resistances of all insulating materials in the walls of a house. Then find the reciprocal of this sum and you have the coefficient of heat transfer.

In one particular house the insulating materials in the walls had the following heat loss resistance ratings: 0.17 for the outside surface, 0.68 for the inside surface, 0.06 for building paper, 11.00 for fiberglass insulation, 0.94 for siding, 0.97 for air space, 0.90 for gypsum. Calculate the coefficient of heat transfer. Round to four decimal places.

(This problem is related to a series of problems in the section on formulas, beginning with problem 42 on page 112.)

37. **Sheet Metal, Heating, and Air Conditioning Specialist *** (III)

One sheet of 20-gauge sheet steel is 0.0359 inch thick. What length of 5/32-inch-diameter rivet is needed to join two sheets of 20-gauge sheet steel? Add 1 1/2 times the diameter of the rivet to the length needed to ensure that a proper rivet head can be formed. (Round final answer to four decimal places.)

38. **Social Worker** (I)

The County Welfare Department will pay child-care expenses for a father on welfare while he is at work or in training for a job.

Social workers must calculate the child-care expenses in advance so that enough money can be set aside by budgeting. How much should be set aside to pay child-care expenses for a father who will need such services for 230 hours per month for 6 1/2 months at $1.50 per hour?

39. Stockbroker (II)

If you sold 250 shares of Exxon at $48 7/8 per share, how many shares of Ford Motor could you buy at $71 3/4 per share?

40. Surveyor (also Civil Engineer) (II)

A condominium development has a flooding problem that requires the installation of a gutter. The surveyor finds the exact point of origin of the gutter by determining its elevation above sea level. The lower end of the gutter is at an elevation of 126.58 feet. Between the lower end and the upper end there must be a grade of 0.8%, meaning the gutter must rise 0.008 feet in elevation for every horizontal foot of gutter. If the total horizontal distance is 80 feet, find the elevation of the upper end of the gutter.

41. Temporary Employment Agency Clerk (II)

An employee worked from 8 A.M. to 4:30 P.M. with 45 minutes off for lunch (unpaid). At $7.50 per hour, what are the employee's wages?

42. Temporary Employment Agency Clerk (II)

Employees who use their own automobiles on the job are reimbursed for gas and depreciation. An employee reported an odometer reading of 19438.6 at the beginning of the day and 19467.2 at the end of the day. How much should the employee be paid if the rate of reimbursement is $0.22 per mile?

43. Wastewater Treatment Operator (I)

The "chlorine demand" is defined as the chlorine dosage minus the residual. Determine the chlorine demand if the dosage is 10.0 mg/l (milligrams per liter) and the residual is 2.4 mg/l.

44. Welder * (I)

A welder finds that 2.083 cubic feet of acetylene gas are needed to make one bracket. How much gas will be needed to make 27 brackets?

When Are We Ever Gonna Have to Use — Averages?

1. **Accountant** (I)

    An accountant for a business is in charge of depreciating company equipment for tax purposes. In the "straight line" method, the total depreciation of an item is averaged over the total number of months or years of depreciation time.

    What would the average monthly depreciation be for a company car costing $12,000 new and depreciated to $0 by the end of the 5-year period?

2. **Airplane Mechanic** (II)

    To estimate the cost of a particular job, a mechanic will often find the average time involved with similar jobs in the past. Suppose a customer wishes to know the cost of an annual inspection for a Bonanza airplane. The mechanic searches the records and finds figures on nine other such inspections. The amounts of time spent on these have been 8, 14, 11, 9, 10, 17, 12, 10, and 9 hours, respectively. Find the average time of these nine jobs and multiply by $18 per hour to calculate the estimated cost.

3. **Airplane Pilot** (I)

    Due to changing wind conditions, a pilot is able to fly at 150 mph for the first third of the flying time of a trip, 175 mph for the middle third of the trip, and 190 mph for the final third. What is the average ground speed for the trip? (Round to the nearest whole number.)

4. **Appliance Store Manager** (I)

    A useful accounting statistic in a retail business is "average inventory." This is defined as the average of "beginning inventory" (goods on hand at the beginning of the quarter) and "ending inventory" (goods on hand at the end of the quarter).

    Find the average inventory for the first quarter of the year if the beginning inventory was $483,000 and the ending inventory was $82,000.

5. **Appraiser (Real Estate)** (II)

    Using the "market approach" to appraisal, real estate appraisers determine the selling prices of other houses in a neighborhood, adjust them for whatever features are different from the house in question, and then compute a weighted average of these prices. The averaging process is weighted according to the similarity of each house to the one being appraised.

In one neighborhood, the adjusted selling prices and weights of four recently sold houses were $179,000 (weighted 0.2), $187,500 (weighted 0.5), $182,000 (weighted 0.2), and $171,000 (weighted 0.1). The weights indicate that the second house is most similar to the house being appraised. Since the sum of the weights is 1.0, to find the weighted average simply multiply each price by its weight, add the four results together, and divide the sum by 4.

6.   **Computer Programmer** (II)

Programmers must give instructions to the computer by writing a general formula that the computer can apply to specific cases. State a formula for finding the average of four numbers a, b, c, and d.

7.   **Controller** (III)

A hospital has 28 beds at $400 per day, 152 beds at $330 per day, 317 beds at $295 per day, 35 beds at $250 per day, and 18 beds at $1100 per day. What is the average cost of a bed to the nearest dollar?

8.   **Fire Fighter** (I)

While fighting a fire, the engineer must perform a pump pressure calculation. One important factor in this calculation is the length of hose extended from the pump. In larger fires, however, more than one hose is connected to the same pump, and the engineer must average the various lengths.

Three hoses connected to the same pump measure 325 feet, 260 feet, and 185 feet. What is their average length?

9.   **Fire Prevention Officer** (II)

Fire prevention personnel must compute statistics to determine how successful they are. Over the past five years, there have been 153 fires in a 23,500-acre section of forest. How many fires would this be per thousand acres? (Round to the nearest tenth.)

10.   **Forestry Recreation Management Officer** (II)

Forestry recreation personnel must keep statistics on the number of vehicles and the number of people entering the national parks.

When Are We Ever Gonna Have to Use This?

If they have reliable statistics on the average number of people per vehicle, then they only have to count vehicles to obtain both of these statistics.

On a day when 223 vehicles entered a park, there were 732 people present.

a. What is the average number of people per vehicle? (Round to the nearest tenth.)

b. Using this figure, how many people would you predict are in the park on a day when 385 vehicles enter?

11.   Hydrologist (III)

A hydrologist wishes to determine the velocity of a stream. She throws an object into the stream and measures the time it takes to travel 200 feet. Then she divides this time into 200 to get the velocity in feet per second. For accuracy, she repeats this process four times and averages the velocities.

What is the average velocity if the times for the four trials are 21 seconds, 23 seconds, 20 seconds, and 23 seconds? (Round to the nearest tenth.)

12.   Income Tax Specialist (I)

A franchise income tax office manager must project the volume of business he will have this year in order to do his hiring and place orders for supplies. As the first step in this calculation, he will compute the average percent of increase in clients of four nearby offices for last year. He will assume that his percent of increase this year will be similar.

Last year the four nearby offices had client increases amounting to 6.4%, 2.7%, 11.5%, and 7.3%. What will he predict his percent of client increase will be this year?

13.   Machinist * (I)

A machinist measured the thickness of a piece of steel five times with a micrometer and then averaged the readings to obtain a precise answer. The five measurements were 0.7841 in., 0.7855 in., 0.7849 in., 0.7844 in., and 0.7851 in. Find the average reading.

14. Meteorologist (III)

Meteorologists calculate average temperatures, rainfall, and wind speed as part of keeping records for a particular area. These records are used to spot changes in weather patterns as well as to inform the public of what to expect.

In one city, the average temperature in June for the past 30 years has been 65.2 degrees. This year the average June temperature was 71.8 degrees. What is the new 31-year average?

15. Motorcycle Sales and Repair (II)

The monthly bike sales for the first five months of the year have been 11, 9, 13, 20, and 8. Assuming the remainder of the year will reflect the monthly average so far, find the monthly average and use it to estimate the sales for the entire year.

16. Optician (II)

A customer chooses a frame that is 71 mm wide. Her eyes are 61 mm apart. How far in from the edge of the frame should the optical centers of the lenses be?

17. Pharmacist (I)

To reduce the dosage of a drug, a pharmacist must first empty the original capsules to find their average weight. Then she can determine how much filler to add to the new capsules so that they will weigh the same as the original ones.

If fifteen capsules weigh a total of 3523 mg, what is the average weight of a capsule to the nearest milligram?

18. Police Officer (II)

Officers are often evaluated on the basis of their activity. This can be measured in terms of average numbers of citations, calls, or investigations.

Officer Larson wrote 276 citations in 64 days, Officer Jones wrote 538 citations in 79 days, and Officer Martinez wrote 312 citations in 54 days.

a. Find the average number of citations per day for each officer and rank them. (Round to the nearest tenth.)

b. Find the average number of citations per day for the three officers combined.

19. Printer (II)

During the past six months a printer has used the following amounts of paper: 6240 lb, 3870 lb, 2592 lb, 7375 lb, 4600 lb, and 6150 lb.

a. Based on a monthly average how much should she order for this month? (Round to the nearest 10 lb.)

b. If she already has 2000 lb in reserve, would this amount plus the answer to part (a) have been enough to handle the peak month of the past six months?

20. Real Estate Agent (I)

A real estate agent wishes to establish a fair rental price for a two-bedroom, one-bath apartment. He finds that the rents charged in eight other similar apartments in the area are: $635, $680, $650, $675, $615, $650, $640, and $650. Based on the average of these, what would be a fair rental price for the apartment? (Round to the nearest multiple of $5.)

21. Stockbroker (I)

Stock market analysts often try to project the earnings of corporations so their brokerage houses can advise clients on which stocks to buy. If several different analysts predict the earnings of the same stock, the broker will use the average of these predictions as a guideline.

Four different analysts have projected the earnings of a certain company to be $6.85, $6.25, $6.40, and $7.10. What average figure would a stockbroker use in advising clients?

22. Travel Agent (III)

A customer is planning to stay 10 nights at the Sheraton Waikiki for $125 per night, 6 nights at the Kona Surf for $140 per night, and 4 nights at the Maui Marriott for $175 per night. He wishes to know the average cost of lodging per night on his Hawaiian vacation. What does the travel agent tell him?

23. Wastewater Treatment Operator (I)

A seven-day average of settleable solids cannot exceed 0.15 ml/l according to the water quality board. During the past seven days, the measurements of concentration have been 0.13, 0.18, 0.21, 0.14, 0.12, 0.11, and 0.15. What was the average? Was it within the limit?

When Are We Ever Gonna Have to Use —
Ratio and Proportion?

1. **Accounting Systems Analyst** (III)

    A city utility bill of $60.60 includes $31.60 for water, $12.40 for sewer, and $16.60 for trash. If the customer makes a partial payment of $24, how much should go toward each department if the payment is distributed proportionally?

2. **Administrator (Shopping Mall)** (I)

    The maintenance bill for the entire shopping center of 180,000 square feet is $45,000 for the quarter. What proportional share does a store of 2400 square feet owe?

3. **Airplane Mechanic (also Airplane Pilot)** (I)

    If a plane uses 20 gallons of gasoline to fly 260 miles, how many gallons will it need to fly 400 miles? (Round to the nearest tenth.)

4. **Airplane Pilot** (III)

    A pilot traveling 175 miles per hour encounters a head wind of 35 knots. If there are 1.15 knots per mph, what will her true speed be in miles per hour? (Round to the nearest mph.)

5. **Appliance Store Manager** (II)

    The ratio of total sales to average inventory is called an "inventory ratio." This ratio tells a retail store manager the number of times her inventory will turn over in a year. By dividing this ratio into 365, she determines how often she needs to restock.

    Find the inventory ratio for an appliance store with total sales of $495,000 and an average inventory of $132,000. Then compute the amount of time each inventory lasts.

6. **Attorney** (I)

    A sampling of recent cases showed the ratio of monthly child support to father's yearly income to be 1:40. If a client makes $38,000 annually, how much should he expect to pay in monthly child support?

7. **Auto Mechanic * (I)**

The compression ratio of a Nissan 300 ZX Turbo is 7.8 to 1. If the compressed volume of one cylinder is 3.868 cu in., what is the expanded volume of the cylinder?

8. **Biologist (Environmental) (III)**

An aerial photo must be made of an area of environmental concern. To be distinguishable, an area 300 feet long in reality must be 1/8 inch long on the photograph.

a. State this ratio in inches to inches.

b. From what altitude must a picture be taken if the camera has a focal length of 0.5 feet?

$$\left(\text{Hint:} \quad \frac{\text{Focal length}}{\text{Altitude}} = \frac{\text{Photo dimension}}{\text{Actual dimension}} \right)$$

9. **Carpet Cleaner (III)**

A certain chemical must be mixed at a ratio of 1:50 (1 part chemical to 50 parts water). A carpet cleaner needs a total of 2 1/2 gallons of solution. How many ounces of each should be added?

10. **Carpet Cleaner (III)**

A special dispensing machine will add 128 parts of water to 1 part of the liquid in the machine. If a certain chemical must be dispensed in the ratio of 1 part chemical for every 448 parts of water, how should the mixture be diluted before it is poured into the machine?

11. **Civil Engineer (III)**

A certain mix of concrete is composed of 94 lb (one sack) of cement, 50 lb of water, 191 lb of sand, and 299 lb of gravel. The final mix of concrete will weigh 151.2 lb/ft³. How many sacks of cement will be needed for a wall with a volume of 1760 ft³?

12. **Civil Engineer (III)**

When constructing a roadway, the civil engineer must set a stake where the outer slope of an embankment will meet the ground.

This tells the equipment operator where to begin the embankment.

The drawing below shows a 40-foot roadway and the right and left embankments. Using the indicated measurements, find the distances X and Y.

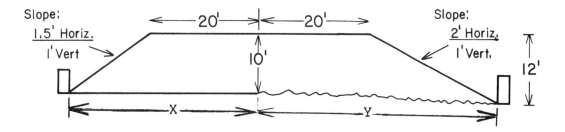

13. Construction Supplies Counter Clerk (II)

A customer desires to mix her own concrete. The clerk knows that the ratio of cement to sand to gravel is 1:3:4. If the customer needs 1000 pounds of dry mix, how many pounds of each ingredient should she use?

14. Contractor (also Architect, Drafter) (I)

The directors of an amusement park wish to build a replica of a town at 5/8 scale. Find the scaled-down dimensions of a building that, in reality, is 40 feet by 58 feet by 10 feet.

15. Controller (Hospital) (I)

The cost of janitorial supplies over an 8-month period has been $943.80. Projected over an entire year, what is the cost likely to be? (Round to the nearest dollar.)

16. Environmental Analyst (II)

Studies show that traffic increases by 650–800 cars per day for every additional 10,000 square feet of commercial business space. What is the range of traffic increase expected from a planned commercial development of 68,500 square feet? (Round to the nearest ten.)

17. **Environmental Analyst** (I)

The ratio of hydrocarbon to nitrogen oxide quantities in the air affects the photochemical reactions that produce smog. The average hydrocarbon emission of an automobile is 5.5 grams per mile, and the average nitrogen oxide emission is 4.7 grams per mile. Express this as a ratio with a second term of 1. (Round to the nearest hundredth.)

18. **Farm Advisor** (I)

It takes 50 seconds to discharge 750 cc from a small sprayer. How long should you spray if you want to discharge only 330 cc?

19. **Farm Advisor** (II)

While calibrating a sprayer, a farmer finds that 19 ounces of spray covers a test plot of 100 square feet. Calculate the discharge rate of the sprayer in gallons per acre. (**Hint:** 1 acre = 43,500 square feet and 1 gallon = 128 ounces.)

20. **Farm Advisor** (III)

A spray rig moving at 3 mph delivers 44 gallons per acre when the nozzles on the rig are 20 inches apart.

a. Suppose the number of nozzles were increased so that they were only 15 inches apart. Find the new delivery rate of the rig.

b. How could this revised delivery rate be achieved by changing the speed of the rig instead of the spacing of the nozzles?

(**Hint:** Both calculations require inverse proportions.)

21. **Forestry Land Management Planner** (I)

In land management different alternatives for development are considered and the best alternative is chosen. One way to measure the values of the different alternatives is by computing their benefit-to-cost ratios.

Two alternative development plans are being considered for a national park. One has benefits worth $1,720,500 and costs of $442,900. The other has benefits of $950,000 and costs of $275,800. Find the benefit-to-cost ratio of each to the nearest hundredth and decide which would be the best plan.

22. Forestry Recreation Management Officer (I)

A survey conducted in the past showed that out of 2500 vehicles traveling along a county highway, 300 turned into a recreational area. Current county data show traffic along that highway to be 3250 vehicles daily. Assuming the same proportion use the recreational area, how many vehicles would this be?

23. Forestry Recreation Management Officer (II)

A forestry survey has determined that an average of 3.3 people occupy each vehicle entering a particular recreational area. In addition, statistics show that each person uses an average of 6 gallons of water per day. Using these figures, calculate the approximate number of vehicles that entered the park on a day when the water meter showed that 2482 gallons of water were used.

24. Industrial Engineer (II)

The term "refrigeration ton" refers to the removal of enough heat to change one ton of water at 32 degrees Fahrenheit into ice in one day. If this amounts to 144 BTU per pound, how many BTU per hour is it?

25. Industrial Engineer (III)

A 10,000-pound uniform payload with base dimensions of 10 feet by 8 feet has a center of gravity centered in the length but offset by 2 feet in the width. How much load is exerted at each corner A, B, C, and D as shown in the drawing?

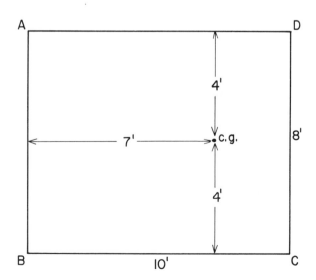

26. **Landscape Architect (also Civil Engineer, Contractor)** (II)

A road must be designed that will travel 4 miles horizontally and drop 2500 feet in elevation. What is the slope of the road as a ratio of horizontal to vertical? (Be sure the units within the ratio match, and round to the nearest tenth.)

27. **Machinist * ** (II)

The speed of a pulley is inversely proportional to its diameter. A 9-inch pulley on a drill press rotates at 1260 rpm. It is belted to a 5-inch pulley on an electric motor. Find the speed of the motor shaft.

28. **Medical Lab Technician** (II)

A basic law of physics states that the concentration of a substance is directly proportional to the intensity of light it absorbs. To find the concentration of substances in bodily fluids, a lab technician use a colorometer to measure the light waves passing through them. He then measures the light waves passing through a substance whose concentration is known (called a "standard"). Finally he sets up the proportion:

$$\frac{\text{Concentration of Standard}}{\text{Absorbance of Standard}} = \frac{\text{Concentration of Unknown}}{\text{Absorbance of Unknown}}$$

In a blood glucose test, the concentration of the standard was 100 mg/dl, the absorbance of the standard was 0.0234, and the absorbance of the unknown was 0.0206. Find the concentration of the unknown.

29. **Motorcycle Sales and Repair** (II)

In a two-cycle engine, gas and oil are mixed together in certain ratios. In a Honda CR 125, the ratio of gas to oil is 20:1. How many ounces of oil must be added to 2 gallons of gas?

30. **Motorcycle Sales and Repair** (I)

The rear sprocket on a bike has 45 teeth while the front sprocket has 15 teeth.

a. What is the ratio of rear to front?

b. For hill climbing the owner wishes to have a 5:1 ratio. If the rear sprocket remains the same, how many teeth should the front sprocket have?

c. If the front sprocket remains the same, how many teeth should the rear sprocket have for a 5:1 ratio?

31. **Nurse** (III)

A doctor orders 20 grains of medicine for a patient. The medicine on hand is in tablets of 250 milligrams each. Given that there are 60 milligrams in 1 grain, how many tablets does the nurse administer?

32. **Nurse** (III)

The doctor orders 1/250 grain for a patient. The nurse has a vial labeled 1/200 grain per cc. If there are 15 minims per cc, how many minims should he give?

33. **Painter** * (I)

If one gallon of paint covers 825 square feet, how much paint is needed to cover 2640 square feet? (Assume the painter cannot purchase a fraction of a gallon.)

34. **Pharmacist** (II)

A certain creme mixture contains 12 grams of creme A, 18.6 grams petrolatum, and 30 grams univase. The pharmacist needs to make a 480-gram mixture containing the same ratio of ingredients. How much of each ingredient should she include?

35. **Pharmacist** (I)

If there are 300 mg morphine in a 360-cc solution, how much morphine should be in a 250-cc solution?

36. **Photographer** (II)

A chemical must be mixed in the ratio of 1 part chemical to 7 parts water. How many ounces of the chemical should be used to obtain a 2-quart mixture?

37. Plumber (also Architect, Drafter) (I)

The scale on a set of plans states that 1/8 inch equals 1 foot. If a water line measures 5 1/2 inches on the plans, what would its actual length be?

38. Political Campaign Manager (I)

There are 28,200 registered Democrats out of 46,500 total registered voters in a district. How many Democrats should be included in a telephone poll of 500 in order to reflect this same proportion?

39. Printer (I)

A particular kind of paper weighs 11 pounds per 500 sheets. How many pounds are needed to run a job of 3200 sheets?

40. Printer (I)

A photograph 6 inches wide and 7 inches high must be reduced to fit in a space 4 1/2 inches wide. How much vertical space will the reduced version require?

41. Printer (III)

In all printing jobs, a certain percentage of pages will be spoiled. Although these cannot be used, the customer must be charged for them. A spoilage chart offers the following information:

Sheets	One Color/Two Sides	Each Additional Color
1000	20% Spoilage	10% Spoilage
2500	15% Spoilage	8% Spoilage

In one particular job, 2200 copies of a brochure must be printed using two colors on two sides. Using linear interpolation in both columns of the chart, find the total spoilage rate expected in this case.

42. Real Estate Agent (I)

If 400 square feet of office space rents for $485 per month, how much will 320 square feet rent for?

43. Real Estate Agent (II)

Five people invest $67,000 in an apartment building in the following amounts:

A — $8,000; B — $18,000; C — $13,000; D — $21,000; E — $7,000

a. If the distribution of cash flow is proportional to the amounts invested, how much will each partner receive out of a $475 total monthly cash flow?

b. If the building is sold in 5 years for a $307,000 net profit, how much of this will each partner receive?

44. Savings and Loan Counselor (III)

ABC Company has a payroll savings plan with a savings and loan. The following employees have contributed to the account in the manner shown:

Employee	Contributed Since	Amount per Month
J.D.	Jan. 1	$ 50
M.S.	July 1	75
S.Q.	July 1	25
S.M.	Sep. 1	100

Based on time and amounts, what fraction of the interest payable on December 31 will each person receive?

45. Savings and Loan Counselor (I)

In structuring certain kinds of loans, banks and savings and loan associations use a figure called "debt service ratio":

$$\text{Debt Service Ratio} = \frac{\text{annual net cash flow}}{\text{annual mortgage payments}}$$

An investor wants to take out a loan to buy an office building. The annual net cash flow on the building is $100,000. The counselor advises the investor that the savings and loan association will require a debt service ratio of 1.25:1. What will be the annual mortgage payments on the loan?

46. Stockbroker (II)

One of the quantitative measures of the strength of a stock is the ratio of its selling price to its earnings per share (price-earnings or PE ratio). A stock with good growth potential will have a high PE ratio, while a troubled stock will have a low PE ratio.

a. Rounded off to the nearest whole number, what is the PE ratio of a stock selling at $87 1/8 and earning $6.36 per share?

b. A cosmetics firm has just announced annual earnings of $3.46 per share. Other cosmetics stocks are selling at an average PE ratio of 9 to 1. Using the same ratio, what is the potential selling price of this stock? (Round to the nearest dollar.)

47. Temporary Employment Agency Clerk (I)

The manager has forecast overall sales of $1.2 million for the coming year. Last year, out of total sales of $975,000, $225,000 occurred in the first quarter. Based on the performance last year and the forecast for this year, what amount of sales should occur in the first quarter of this year? (Round to the nearest thousand.)

48. Veterinarian (II)

A certain drug must be administered at a rate of 10 mg per pound of body weight per day. If a 45-pound dog is given this medication in three doses per day, how much should each dose contain?

When Are We Ever Gonna Have to Use — Percent?

1.   Accountant (II)

Management wishes to know how rapidly they are spending the budget for a particular project. With 6 weeks left on an 18-week project, they have used $45,000 of a $62,000 budget. Compare the percent of time remaining with the percent of budget remaining. (Round to the nearest tenth.)

2.   Administrator (Shopping Mall) (I)

A store is charged a monthly rent of $1350 or 6% of sales, whichever is greater.

a. What is the rent if the store's monthly sales total $17,500?

b. What is the rent for monthly sales of $28,650?

3.   Advertising Agent (II)

An agent has expenses totaling $1305.75 for a particular job. Her fee is 15% of the gross (expenses plus fee). What is the total bill she presents to the client?

4.   Airline Passenger Service Agent (III)

To determine the cost of shipping live animals, airline personnel first must calculate the dimensional weight of the kennel (see page 96, problem 2). The rest of the calculation may require several steps involving different percents.

For example, to ship an animal from Santa Barbara to St. Louis, two different airlines are involved. For the Santa Barbara to Los Angeles flight, the rate for an animal is 200% of the normal air freight rate. The normal rate is 44 cents per pound of dimensional weight or a $22 minimum. For the L.A. to St. Louis flight, the rate for an animal is 110% of the normal air freight rate. The normal rate is 91 cents per pound of dimensional weight or a $30 minimum. Finally, a 5% tax is added to the total shipping charge.

Find the cost of shipping a dog from Santa Barbara to St. Louis if the dimensional weight of the kennel is:

a. 116 lb

b. 24.5 lb

(For added practice, work this same problem using the result of problem 2 on page 96.)

5. **Airplane Mechanic** (I)

An airplane's cruising speed of 240 knots is increased by 12%. What is its new cruising speed?

6. **Airplane Pilot (also Airplane Mechanic)** (I)

How much horsepower is a 160-hp engine using at 65% efficiency?

7. **Appliance Store Manager** (II)

One way in which a retail store manager uses percent is to evaluate the effectiveness of advertising. The following chart compares the reasons customers entered a store on a normal day to those on a day during a newspaper ad campaign.

Reason	Normal	Ad Day
Advertising	18	46
Previous purchase	14	12
Through friend	21	24
Phone book	26	21
Driving by	7	4
Other	9	8
Total	95	115

a. What percent of the total customers came into the store because of advertising on the normal day?

b. What percent of the total customers came into the store because of advertising on the ad day?

c. What was the percent increase of total customers between the normal day and the ad day?

d. What was the percent increase in the advertising category between the normal day and the ad day?

8. **Appliance Store Manager** (II)

Percent is also involved in determining the selling price of items in a retail store. These are based either on a percent markup over the cost (profit margin) or, during a sale, a percent discount from the normal selling price.

Suppose the costs for some items in an appliance store were as follows: dishwasher, $360; washing machine, $335; television, $422.

  a. If the manager wishes to have a 35% profit margin on these items, what should the selling prices be?

  b. During the end-of-the-month clearance, these same items are then discounted 15% from the selling prices. What are the resulting sale prices?

  c. What percent profit margin does the manager have with the sale prices?

9. **Appliance Store Manager** (I)

An important statistic for the owner-manager of a retail store is the "ownership equity." Ownership equity is the percent of total assets that is net worth. If net worth is $171,358 and total assets are $598,784, what is the ownership equity?

10. **Appliance Store Manager** (I)

Retail stores often prepare their budgets according to percent figures using national averages as a guideline. The national averages for retail stores grossing over $1,000,000 indicate that total pay for salespeople should be 5.6% of net sales. If a store projects net sales of $1,250,000 in the coming year, how much should be allotted for salespeople?

11. **Architect (also Civil Engineer)** (I)

The building code states that, because of heat loss, the window area of a building cannot exceed 20% of the floor area. For floor space of 1350 square feet, would 275 square feet of windows satisfy the code?

12. Attorney (II)

At the time of a divorce settlement a couple has $100,000 worth of personal property and a house worth $240,000. If the husband takes $80,000 of the property and the wife takes the other $20,000, what percent ownership of the house should she be given for the settlement to come out even?

13. Auto Mechanic (II)

A tail lamp assembly retails for $78.48 and wholesales for $47.09. One parts house offers the assembly to the mechanic at a 35% discount off the retail price, while another source offers it at a 25% markup over the wholesale price. Which is the better deal?

14. Carpenter (I)

A certain carpenter marks up the cost of materials 5% when charging the customer. If his cost for materials was $263.78, what would he charge his customer?

15. Construction Supplies Counter Clerk (also Contractor) (I)

A contractor's bill for one month is $1743.90. If she pays in full by the end of the month, she is entitled to a 2% discount. How much would she owe with this discount?

16. Contractor (also Savings and Loan Counselor) (III)

When a builder takes out a construction loan, he pays interest on the money only as he spends it. On a loan of $12,000, the builder has stated he will spend 20% the first month, another 50% the second month, and the remaining 30% during the third month. Based on the cumulative total spent, how much monthly interest does he owe at the end of each of the three months if the interest rate is 14% annually?

17. Controller (Hospital) (III)

An FICA (Social Security) tax of 7.51% and an SDI (State Disability Insurance) deduction of 1.2% are charged against an employee's wages. If her total monthly wages were $1538.46, what would her paycheck be after FICA and SDI deductions as well as withholding tax deductions of $245.80?

18. **Controller (Hospital)** (II)

A manufacturer gives the hospital a 2% discount if it pays its bills within 10 days of the billing date. The manufacturer also charges 1.5% interest per month for payment received after 30 days of the billing date. The hospital receives a bill of $1432.60 on August 3. How much do they owe if they pay on:

a. August 8?

b. August 24?

c. September 18?

d. December 20? (Be sure to compound the interest monthly.)

19. **Dietician** (I)

A doctor prescribes a diet of 2500 calories per day for a patient. She specifies that 40% of the calories must be carbohydrates, 35% must be fat, and 25% must be protein. Compute the number of calories in each category.

20. **Dietician** (III)

Carbohydrates contain 4 calories per gram, fat contains 9 calories per gram, and protein contains 4 calories per gram. Of carbohydrates, 100% of the total weight in grams breaks down into glucose. Of fat, 10% of the total weight in grams breaks down into glucose. Of protein, 58% of the total weight breaks down into glucose. Use the answers to problem 19 to determine the total available glucose in grams for the indicated diet.

21. **Electrical Inspector** (II)

The electrical code specifies how to calculate the net load in watts for different types of appliances and lights. This information is then used to determine such things as current requirements.

For example, to compute the net load for general lighting, small appliances, and laundry in a home, add 100% of the first 3000 watts to 35% of the remainder. This formula is used because these items are not demanding electricity on a constant basis.

Determine the net load if the total load for general lighting, small appliances, and laundry is 8000 watts.

22. Electrical Inspector (III)

As an alternative to the method in problem 21, the code states that if the total load is given in kilowatts, the net load can be computed by adding 100% of the first 10 kw to 40% of the remainder.

a. If the total load is 37.9 kw, what is the net load?

b. Current in amperes is equal to the load in watts divided by voltage. Use the result of part (a) to determine if a 100-ampere service would be sufficient for 230 volts.

23. Electrician * (I)

An electrical resistor is rated at 500 ohms plus or minus 3%. What is the actual range of resistance?

24. Fire Prevention Officer (I)

The fire prevention officer must determine the best allocation of the budget for preventing forest fires. The first step is to determine which types of fires are most common so the budget focuses on prevention of these fires. Percent plays a large part in this determination.

a. In the central region last year, 24 out of 77 human-caused fires were incendiary. What percent were incendiary?

b. The prevention officer wishes to reduce the number of incendiary fires by 12% of the 5-year average. If the 5-year average is 28, what would the maximum number have to be this year to achieve this goal?

25. Forestry Recreation Management Officer (I)

Groups that use a large area of U.S. Forest Service lands are charged a yearly fee equal to 5% of the land value. How much would the Boy Scouts be charged for a 6-acre campsite if the land is valued at $2200 per acre?

26. Forestry Recreation Management Officer (III)

Recreation management officers must compute the number of people using a particular area without making an on-site count. To do this they use statistical data based on region-wide averages to make a reasonable estimate. Following are examples of such data:

- Pine Haven, a 75-unit campground, has a "high-use" season of 95 days.

- 65.8% of all units are occupied during the high-use season.

- High-use season represents 85% of the total annual use of a campground.

- There are on average 5.28 "visitor-days" for each occupied unit. (This means 5.28 visitors per day of occupation.)

- 37% of all campground use occurs during the day. 63% of all use occurs at night.

- Nighttime use consists of 23.7% auto camping, 47.7% trailer camping, and 28.6% tent camping.

Use the above data to answer the following questions:

a. What is the total number of occupied units at Pine Haven during the high-use season?

b. What is the total number of occupied units at Pine Haven during the entire year?

c. What is the total number of visitor-days per year for daytime use?

d. How many visitor-days are involved annually in nighttime camping? Break this figure down into number of auto, trailer, and tent visitor-days.

27. **Geologist** (III)

A geologist was asked to evaluate the impact of site construction on the infiltration of rain to the groundwater supply. The geologist estimated that 5% of the total rainfall would normally infiltrate to the groundwater supply. After construction none of the rainfall falling on the site would infiltrate. If the site totals 150 acres, and the average yearly precipitation is 6 inches, determine the total annual loss of groundwater in acre-feet. (An acre-foot is equal to a one-foot depth of water covering an acre of land.)

28. **Hydrologist** (I)

In describing the characteristics of a stream, a hydrologist might wish to state the percent of increase or decrease in stream flow between two points.

If the flow at point A is 7 feet per second, and the flow at point B is 5 feet per second, what percent of the flow is lost between A and B?

29. **Income Tax Specialist** (I)

Under current income tax law, you may deduct only 80% of your total business expenses for meals and entertainment. If you spent $872.68 for meals and $528.25 for entertainment, how much could you deduct from your taxes?

30. **Income Tax Specialist** (II)

To deduct medical expenses, they must exceed 7.5% of your adjusted gross income. Then you may deduct only the amount over 7.5%.

If your adjusted gross income was $19,438, and medical expenses in excess of insurance coverage amounted to $1746, how much can you deduct?

31. **Income Tax Specialist** (II)

For a taxpayer with $21,000 of gross income, child-care expenses are a 24% tax credit. This means that 24% of the cost of child care may be subtracted directly from the tax owed.

If the tax owed was $1611 before deducting this credit, and child-care expenses were $1450, what was the final tax bill?

32. **Income Tax Specialist** (II)

The franchise manager of an income tax service decides to spend 90% of her advertising budget over the four weeks just prior to the tax deadline. 60% of this will be spent during the first and fourth weeks, while the other 40% will be spent during the second and third weeks. If the total advertising budget is $1800, compute the amount to be spent during the second and third weeks.

33. Income Tax Specialist (II)

A single person having a retirement plan at work and earning up to $25,000 annually may contribute a maximum of $2000 annually to an IRA (Individual Retirement Account). However, if one's income exceeds $25,000, this contribution must be reduced by 20% of the difference between the salary and $25,000. How much can a single person earning $31,200 contribute annually to an IRA?

34. Industrial Engineer (III)

A plant is currently operating at 85% of maximum output, and it is shipping $18,000,000 worth of equipment per year.

a. How much equipment can be shipped at maximum capacity?

b. How much equipment can be shipped at maximum capacity plus 10% overtime?

c. How much can be shipped at maximum capacity plus one-half of a second shift if the second shift is 10% less productive than the first shift?

d. If 4000 hours per week are needed to meet the current needs, how many hours will be needed to ship $25,000,000 worth of equipment per year?

35. Industrial Engineer (II)

The reject rate on parts is usually 5%. Last week 47 parts were inspected and 3 were rejected. Was the rate last week higher or lower than normal? By what percent?

36. Insurance Agent (II)

A pension plan is being set up for a 50-year-old executive who, at age 65, will draw a monthly benefit equal to 30% of her present monthly salary. If her present annual salary is $150,000, what will her monthly pension be?

37. Insurance Agent (II)

A 21-year-old single male with a "B" average in college drives a 1986 VW van 15,000 miles per year. This puts him in insurance class B2. Here he is entitled to a 25% discount on liability, medical, comprehensive, and collision, but not on towing or uninsured motorists coverage. Following is a list of the semi-annual premiums for each coverage before the discount is applied. Determine his total annual premium with the discount.

Liability	$217.00
Uninsured Motorists	10.40
Medical	15.00
Comprehensive	56.00
Collision	213.00
Towing	5.00

38. Interior Decorator (III)

For some jobs the calculations for total cost automatically include materials and labor but not sales tax. In order to find the sales tax, the decorator must separate the cost of materials according to a pre-defined percentage. If the pre-tax cost of a job is $688, and the job is known to be 37% materials, what would the total cost be after 6.5% sales tax is applied to the cost of materials?

39. Interior Decorator (I)

To order material for draperies, a decorator takes the measurement of the window and adds "100% fullness" (additional material to provide for pleats). If a window measures 112 inches wide, what total width of material would the decorator order?

40. Landscape Architect (also Civil Engineer) (I)

Architects are often concerned with the slope of land. This may be expressed as a ratio of horizontal change to vertical change, such as 2 to 1. In other cases it may be expressed as a percent of vertical to horizontal. For example, a 2 to 1 slope would be expressed as 50%. Change each of the following ratios to percent slopes.

a. 3 to 1

b. 4 to 1

c. 8.4 to 1

d. 27 to 1

41. **Librarian** (III)

Planning shelf space is one of the major tasks of a librarian. In the past five years, the number of volumes in a city library has been as follows: 38,250; 42,363; 46,850; 51,925; 57,793.

a. Find the average yearly percent of growth during this period to the nearest tenth of a percent. (**Hint:** Find each yearly percent of increase and average these.)

b. Based on the answer to part (a), predict the number of volumes the library will have next year. (Round to the nearest ten.)

42. **Machinist** * (I)

Specifications call for a bolt to be 3.125 inches long. If the finished bolt measures 3.121 inches, what is the percent error to the nearest hundredth?

43. **Masonry Contractor** * (I)

On the basis of past experience, a contractor expects to find 4.5% broken bricks in every truckload. If she orders 2000 bricks, will she probably have enough to complete a job requiring 1900 bricks?

44. **Medical Lab Technician** (I)

Lab technicians are concerned with the number of white blood cells called "eosinophils." One method of counting eosinophils was explained in problem 18 on page 13. As a way of double-checking the count, a lab technician can also count the total number of white blood cells (WBC) per cubic millimeter and use the result of a WBC differential count that gives the percent of eosinophils.

If the WBC count reveals 5900 WBC per cubic millimeter, and the WBC differential shows 8% eosinophils, how many eosinophils per cubic millimeter should there be?

45. **Meteorologist** (I)

Meteorologists divide the horizon circle into 360 degrees. North is at 0 or 360, east is at 90, south is at 180, and west is at 270. If one cloud mass extends from 10 degrees to 130 degrees, and another extends from 240 to 300 degrees, what percent of the horizon is obscured?

46. Motorcycle Sales and Repair (II)

For a Vespa bike, the amount of oil added to the gas tank should be 5% of the amount of gas. How many ounces of oil must be added to 1.5 gallons of gas?

47. Painter (I)

To double-check their estimate of the cost of a job, many painters apply the rule of thumb that materials should constitute 20% of the total cost. If the total estimate for a job comes to $825, about how much should the materials cost?

48. Payroll Supervisor (I)

Good cost accounting practice requires allocating expense to certain projects, accounts, or burden centers. Suppose there are three burden centers that must absorb a total cost of $20,000. The first center must absorb 45%, the second 35%, and the third 20%. What is the cost absorbed by each center?

49. Pharmacist (I)

A pharmacist needs a 1% solution of a certain medication. She has a mixture available that contains 1.0 grams of the substance in 20 cc of solution. How much buffer should she add to obtain the desired concentration? (**Note:** The percent is calculated from grams divided by cc.)

50. Plumber (County Inspector) (III)

The seepage pit for a septic tank must drain water within a certain amount of time in order to meet code regulations. When the county inspector performs the seepage tests, he must repeatedly record the time it takes for six inches of water to drain until the times for two successive tests do not vary by more than 20%.

If six successive tests resulted in times of 6 minutes, 10 minutes, 14 minutes, 16 minutes, 18 minutes, and 19 minutes, which test should have been the last one?

51. Police Officer (I)

Police officers must keep careful statistics on crime to evaluate their own performance and to keep the public informed. In

December of this year there were 506 arrests made in a city. In December of last year there were 497 arrests. What was the percent of increase to the nearest tenth?

52. Political Campaign Manager (III)

The fund-raising responsibility of each district is proportional to the percent of total voter income contained in the district. For example, if a certain district has a voter income equal to 2% of the state income, the party would expect the district to supply 2% of the campaign funds.

a. Data shows that your state has 820,000 Republicans with an average income of $26,500. Your district has 7200 registered Republicans with an average income of $28,000. To the nearest hundredth, what percent of the state fund-raising total should your district supply?

b. Suppose the fund-raising goal for the entire state is $950,000. Use your answer to part (a) to compute the amount of money your district should supply. (Round to the nearest hundred.)

53. Printer (II)

A customer receives a 3% discount on the total cost for ordering at least 20,000 forms. The cost per thousand is $440. What would the discounted price be for 27,000 forms?

54. Printer (I)

A customer orders 2000 printed sheets. The printer expects a 25% spoilage rate for this type of job. How many sheets should actually be printed?

55. Publishing House Order Department Manager (II)

Agents and book dealers receive a 15% discount for handling 10 to 50 copies of the same book. What would the agent pay for 37 copies of a book regularly priced at $9.30 per copy?

56. Publishing House Production Manager (II)

The total bill for typesetting a book is $2502. Because of errors by the author, 324 lines must be re-set at a cost of $0.85 per line. The author must pay for all costs that exceed 10% of the typesetting bill. How much must the author pay?

57. Publishing House Production Manager (III)

The process of setting a price for a book involves several percent calculations. Following is a worked example of the process and then a problem for you to solve.

A certain book costs $5.44 per copy to produce. The author receives a 10% royalty on the first 500 copies and 12.5% after that. The book is expected to sell 2200 copies. Multiplying 0.1 by 500, 0.125 by 1700 (2200 − 500), adding them and dividing by 2200, we get an average author's royalty of approximately 11.9%. To this we add a 6% profit for the publisher for a total profit margin of 17.9%. This means that the cost of $5.44 per copy must represent 82.1% of the selling price. This makes the selling price about $6.63 per copy.

Another book costs $12.48 per copy to produce. The author receives a 12% royalty on the first 1500 copies and 14% after that. The book is expected to sell 6000 copies. The publisher needs a profit of 7%. Determine the selling price of the book.

58. Real Estate Agent (II)

An agent sells a property for $220,000. The broker takes a commission of 3%, out of which the agent receives 60%. How much does the agent receive?

59. Real Estate Agent (II)

The market value of a property is $198,500. Property tax in the area is assessed at 25% of market value. The tax rate is $8.35 per $100 assessed valuation. Find the total property tax.

60. Real Estate Agent (II)

A woman bought 4 lots for $48,000 each. She then subdivided them into a total of 7 lots that sold for $33,000 each. What was her percent of profit to the nearest tenth?

61. Real Estate Agent (III)

A lot was listed for $53,600. The seller agreed to pay an 8.5% commission to the agent. Later the owner agreed to accept an offer 5% less than the listed price when the agent reduced his commission to 6%. What was the total commission paid to the agent under the revised deal?

62. Real Estate Agent (III)

A $12,000 loan is to be repaid at $100 per month plus 15% of the unpaid balance. Find the payments for the first three months. (**Note:** 15% is the annual interest rate, and the unpaid balance refers to the amount unpaid before the current payment.)

63. Savings and Loan Counselor (II)

A self-employed customer wishes to invest as much money as possible into a retirement account. The savings and loan counselor advises the customer to open a two-plan Keough account consisting of a money purchase pension plan and a profit sharing plan. Under the law, self-employed individuals may contribute a maximum of 20% of their net income, and then divide it so that 60% of the contribution goes to the profit sharing plan and 40% goes to the money purchase pension plan. With a net income of $28,400, how much should the customer contribute to each plan?

64. Savings and Loan Counselor (II)

A customer wishes to borrow $30,000, make monthly payments of interest only, and pay the full amount of the principal at the end of the term. If the interest rate is 12% annually, what are the monthly payments for a five-year term?

65. Social Worker (III)

To determine food stamp allotment for qualifying individuals, the following procedure is used:

- Take 80% of gross monthly income.

- Subtract $102 from this result. (This is a standard deduction for medical expenses, transportation, etc.)

- Divide by 2.

- Take this result or $152, whichever is smaller, and subtract it from the result of the second step. This is the "adjusted income."

- Find the adjusted income on the food stamp chart and read the benefit.

Find the adjusted income if the gross monthly income is:

a. $595

b. $475

66. Stockbroker (II)

A client interested in mutual funds wanted a fund that would be as safe as possible in a "bear" (down) market. The broker looked up the net asset values of three different funds at the beginning and the end of a recent bear market cycle that lasted from January 15 to May 3. The results are summarized in the following chart:

Fund	Price on 1/15	Price on 5/3
Aggressive Growth	$37.38	$34.72
Growth and Income	10.27	9.84
Income	12.23	12.00

Compute the percent decrease of each fund and determine which one weathered the bear market best.

67. Stockbroker (II)

Many stocks pay a dividend to the shareholder. Since the dividend represents a certain dollar amount per share of stock, it is difficult to compare dividend returns to each other or to the returns of other investments. For this reason the stockbroker will often convert the dividend into a percent of the price of the stock.

a. Which would produce a better return—a passbook savings account paying 5.5%, or a stock selling for $20 per share and paying a dividend of $1.15 per share?

b. Which produces a higher percent return—a stock selling for $24 7/8 and paying a $1.84 dividend per share, or a stock selling for $15 3/4 and paying a $1.20 dividend?

68. Stockbroker (III)

In recommending investment in a tax-free municipal bond, the broker must compute the "effective yield" of the bond based on the client's tax bracket. For example, a 6% federally tax-exempt bond has an effective yield of 8 1/3% for a client in the 28% tax bracket because a taxable investment of 8 1/3% yields only 6% after federal taxes: $0.06 \div (1.00 - 0.28) = 0.0833$.

Calculate the effective yield of the following tax-free bonds for clients in the given tax brackets. (Round to the nearest 0.1%.)

a. 7.5% bond; 28% bracket

b. 8% bond; 15% bracket

c. 8.5% bond, exempt from federal and state taxes; 28% federal bracket, 8% state bracket

69. **Stockbroker** (II)

Many clients have margin accounts, which means they do not have to come up with all the cash when buying securities. Normally a brokerage will loan up to 50% of the value of the securities.

Suppose a client wished to buy 200 shares of stock selling for $20 per share. She would pay $2000 on margin and borrow the other $2000 from the broker. If the stock went up in value to $30 per share, her borrowing power would increase to 50% of the present value less what she has already borrowed. Based on these figures, what additional amount can she borrow?

70. **Technical Researcher** (II)

To determine the estimated cost of a project, research firms have developed standard methods in which the cost of each item is based on a percent of other items.

Consider the following facts about a project:

a. The professional personnel salaries will be $55,000.

b. The cost of secretarial work will be 30% of the professional personnel salaries.

c. The cost of overhead will be 100% of the total salaries (professional plus secretarial).

d. The cost of independent research will be 4% of overhead.

e. The cost of the bid and proposal will be 14.6% of overhead.

Find the cost of items b, c, d, and e, and the total cost of the project.

71. Travel Agent (I)

An agent books a $650 hotel stay on which she receives a 7% commission. How much is her commission?

72. Veterinarian (II)

A blood test reveals that a dog is 10% dehydrated. The total fluid reservoir needed by the dog is equal to 30% of its weight. How much fluid must be replaced if the dog weighs 78 pounds?

73. Wastewater Treatment Operator (II)

The chlorine dosage of water being treated must be 0.001%. If the flow of water is 600,000 gallons per day, how many pounds of chlorine must be added? (**Hint:** Water weighs 8.34 pounds per gallon.)

74. Wastewater Treatment Operator (III)

It is a well-known fact in this field that 10,000 milligrams per liter (mg/l) equals a 1% solution. Using this fact, other percents can be computed when necessary.

Convert 250 mg/l to a percent solution.

75. Welder * (I)

If hard solder is 68% tin, how many pounds of tin are needed to make 54 pounds of solder?

When Are We Ever Gonna Have to Use — Statistical Graphing?

1.   **Airplane Pilot (also Airplane Mechanic)** (I)

Before taking off, either the pilot or the mechanic for an airplane (particularly a small plane) must determine whether the center of gravity of the plane falls within safe limits. Sometimes this is done with the aid of the graph below:

Graph 1
Safety Envelope for Center of Gravity

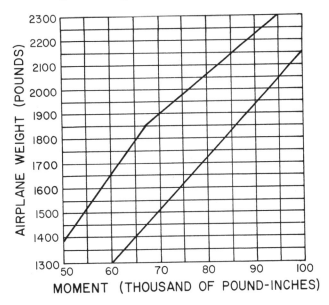

a. Does a weight of 1950 pounds and a moment of 88,600 pound-inches fall within the safety envelope (between the two lines) on Graph 1?

b. Does a weight of 1820 pounds and a moment of 62,000 pound-inches fall within the safety envelope?

2. Highway Patrol Officer (III)

Highway patrol officers must be able to read complex graphs such as the skid-speed chart on page 55 (Graph 2). This information is used to establish fault at the scene of an accident.

To determine the speed a vehicle was traveling, find the skid distance along the left vertical axis. Then move horizontally until you hit the proper coefficient of friction line. Finally, follow straight down and read the speed in miles per hour along the bottom horizontal axis.

Determine the speed in miles per hour for the following skid lengths and friction coefficients:

a. 150-foot skid, coefficient of 30%

b. 45-foot skid, coefficient of 70%

c. 330-foot skid, coefficient of 50%

d. 115-foot skid, coefficient of 40%

3. Highway Patrol Officer (III)

To determine the speed of a vehicle leaving a centrifugal skid mark, the officer lays out a 50-foot chord across the arc of the skid. Then she measures the distance in inches from the middle of the chord to the outside of the arc (the middle ordinate). Next she finds this number on the right side of Graph 2 (page 55) and moves horizontally to the left until she hits the proper coefficient of friction line. Finally, she follows straight down and reads the speed in miles per hour along the bottom horizontal axis.

Determine the speed in miles per hour for the following middle ordinates and friction coefficients:

a. 36-inch ordinate, 70% coefficient

b. 6 1/2-inch ordinate, 40% coefficient

c. 11 1/2-inch ordinate, 50% coefficient

When Are We Ever Gonna Have to Use This?

Graph 2
Skid – Speed Chart

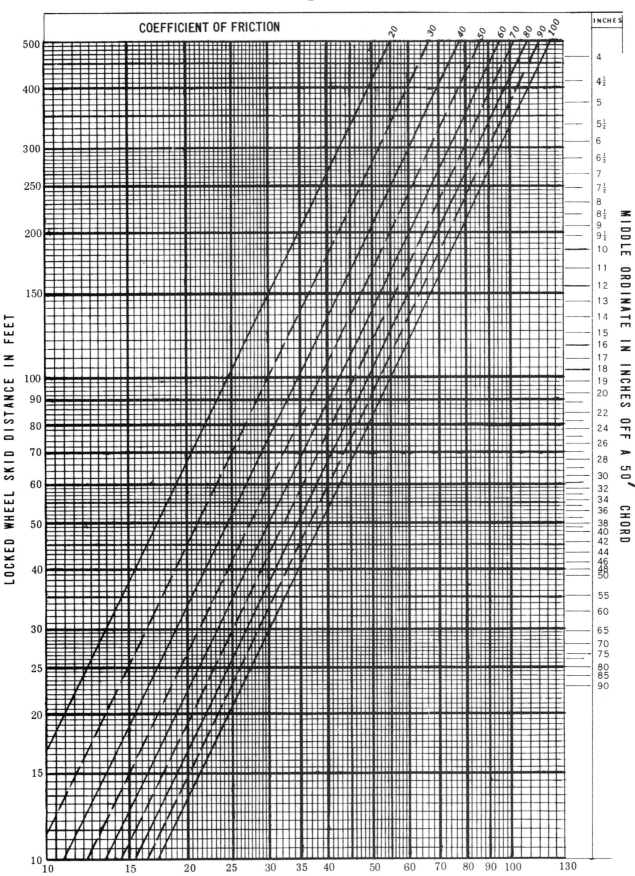

4. **Industrial Engineer** (II)

The product cost in a computer manufacturing plant is 80% material, 12% production labor, 6.8% test labor, and 1.2% inspection labor. Make a circle graph showing these elements of product cost.

5. **Medical Lab Technician** (I)

To measure the concentration of an unknown substance, a standard with a known concentration is normally used, and a proportion is set up to compute the concentration of the unknown. (See problem 28 on page 30.) Sometimes the standard is so unstable, however, that instead of measuring the standard each time, a one-time standard curve is set up from which the technician can read all future unknowns. A sample curve might look like Graph 3 below:

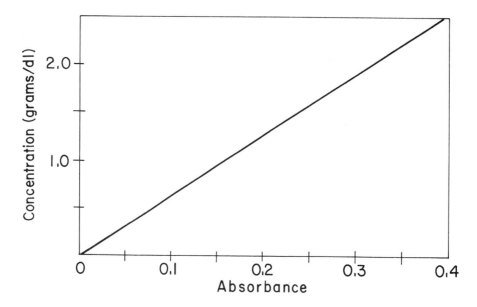

Graph 3
Concentration of an Unknown

a. If the absorbance of the unknown is 0.30, what is the concentration of the unknown? (Estimate to the nearest 0.1.)

b. If the absorbance of the unknown is 0.10, what is its concentration?

When Are We Ever Gonna Have to Use This?

6. **Meteorologist** (II)

Graph 4 below shows the total monthly precipitation measured at a weather station. Use it to answer these questions:

Graph 4
Total Monthly Rainfall

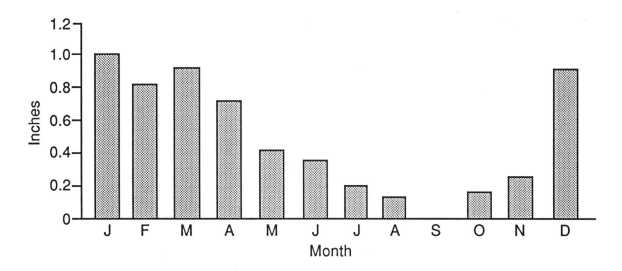

a. During which month is rainfall the highest?

b. During which month is rainfall the lowest?

c. What is the total annual rainfall at the station? (Try to estimate the total for each month to the nearest 0.05 in.)

7. **Plumber * (II)**

Graph 5 on page 58 shows the water demand for different numbers of fixture units. Use it to answer the following questions.

a. In general, do systems with flush valves demand more or less water than flush tanks?

b. What is the demand for 20 fixture units in a predominantly flush valve system? (Estimate to the nearest 5 GPM.)

c. How many gallons per minute (GPM) are required by 190 fixture units in a predominantly flush tank system?

d. What is the maximum number of fixture units you could accommodate with a supply of 45 gallons per minute in a predominantly flush valve system?

e. What is the maximum number of fixture units you could accommodate with a supply of 25 gallons per minute in a predominantly flush tank system?

Graph 5
Demand Load for Water Systems

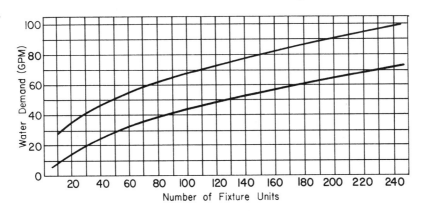

The upper curve is for a predominantly flush valve system.
The lower curve is for a predominantly flush tank system.

8.   Police Officer (I)

The police department must make periodic reports to the city council. These reports make use of statistical graphs illustrating crime and traffic data. Use Graphs 6, 7, and 8 on page 59 to answer the following questions.

a. In which year were total collisions the highest?

b. Did personal injuries peak at this same time? What about fatalities?

c. During which year were fatalities the lowest?

d. During which year did total collisions and fatalities show their largest increase over the previous year?

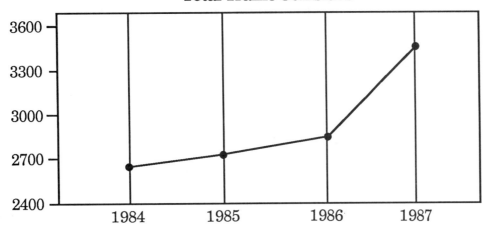

Graph 6
Total Traffic Collisions

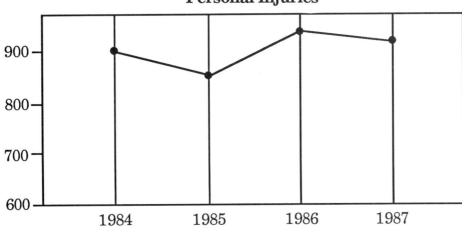

Graph 7
Personal Injuries

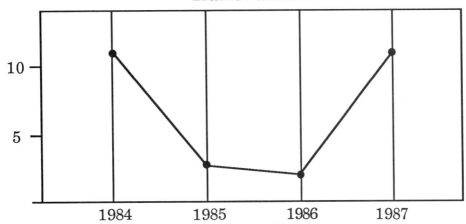

Graph 8
Traffic Fatalities

9.   Real Estate Agent (II)

Graphs are sometimes used to analyze the potential return on individual properties in real estate. Graph 9 below shows the potential sale price of an apartment building as it varies with rent increase and different rates of return.

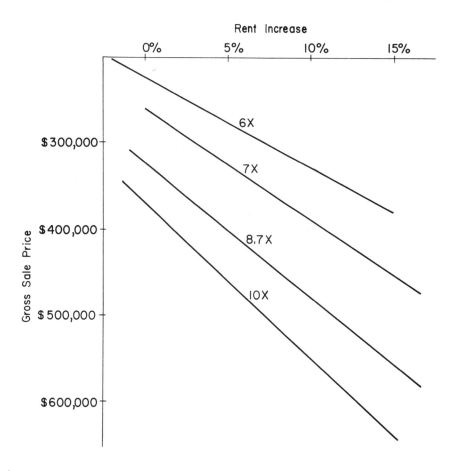

Graph 9
Sale Price Versus Rent Increase

Find the potential gross sale price for the following situations. Estimate the price to the nearest $25,000:

a. 7× return and 5% rent increase

b. 10× return and 10% rent increase

c. 8.7× return and 7.5% rent increase

d. 6× return and 15% rent increase

10.   Temporary Employment Agency Clerk (III)

The manager of a temporary employment agency measured the success of the business by drawing a triple line graph. See if you can duplicate it given the following information:

The vertical axis represents "gross profit per staff salary dollar" (GP/SS). It goes from 0 to 5. The horizontal axis represents time, going from week 1 to week 8. The three lines on the graph should illustrate the data in these charts:

Week	GP/SS This Year	GP/SS Last Year	GP/SS Goal
1	$2.40	$2.20	$2.80
2	3.40	3.00	2.80
3	3.80	3.30	2.80
4	3.40	3.70	2.80
5	2.70	3.20	2.80
6	3.30	2.70	2.80
7	4.70	4.20	2.80
8	4.10	4.60	2.80

When Are We Ever Gonna Have to Use — Miscellaneous Other Topics?

Such as Quick Computation . . .

1. **Airplane Pilot** (III)

   Your altitude is 8000 feet, your speed is 180 mph, and you can descend at 500 feet per minute. How far from your destination should you begin to descend?

2. **Environmental Analyst** (II)

   While discussing an LNG (liquified natural gas) terminal over the phone, an environmental analyst had to solve this problem mentally:

   If 150 ships carrying 130,000 cubic meters of liquified natural gas each unloaded at an LNG terminal, how many total cubic meters of gas would be deposited? Your estimate should be within 500,000 of the precise answer.

Or Rounding . . .

(**Note:** Many of the other problems in this collection involve rounding skills. Here are some problems involving rounding alone.)

3. **Appliance Store Manager** (I)

   Suppose that air conditioners were available in BTU increments of 2000 beginning with 3000 BTUs (3000, 5000, 7000, etc.). Give the closest-sized air conditioners that would fit rooms with each of the following needs:

   a. 7800

   b. 2400

   c. 16,200

   d. 14,100

   e. 6300

4. **Auditor** (I)

In auditing, all amounts are rounded to the nearest dollar. All $0.50 remainders are rounded to the nearest *even* dollar.

Round each of the following amounts as an auditor would.

   a. $7.85

   b. $12.26

   c. $13.50

   d. $188.50

   e. $60.90

5. **Fire Fighter** (II)

Calculations such as nozzle flows can be off by as much as 15 pounds per square inch (psi) without affecting other calculations, such as friction loss. Thus, to simplify calculations, nozzle flow may be rounded as long as it remains within 15 psi of the precise figure.

Round each of the following to the nearest multiple of 25. Is each answer within 15 psi of the original figure?

   a. 266 psi

   b. 312 psi

   c. 238 psi

   d. 329 psi

6. **Medical Lab Technician** (I)

A Coulter cell counter gives a digital readout that must rounded to the nearest hundredth for reporting. Give the rounded figures for each of the following readouts:

   a. 5.438

   b. 5.732

   c. 6.003

   d. 5.555

Or Number Bases Other Than Ten ...

7. **Data Processor (also Computer Programmer, Technical Researcher)** (II)

   Determine the location of a core map if the starting location is 1AB0 and the offset is 3C0 (both base 16). (**Hint:** Find their sum. Answer should be in base 16.)

8. **Data Processor (also Computer Programmer, Technical Researcher)** (III)

   The starting location of a program is 9CEC6, and the program stopped at 9D974 (both base 16). How many steps into the program was it when it terminated? Give the answer in base 10.

9. **Data Processor (also Computer Programmer, Technical Researcher)** (I)

   Control Data computers store information in locations numbered in octal (base 8). Find the octal form of the 93rd location.

10. **Technical Researcher** (II)

   The Landsat satellite, which is used to study the earth's natural resources, must be able to discern 250 shades of brightness. The picture is then sent to the ground by a radio wave carrying a series of binary digits. How many digits are required to transmit all 250 shades of brightness?

Or Scientific Notation ...

11. **Electrical Engineer** (III)

   An electrical engineer simplified the large numbers in the following calculation by using scientific notation:

   A school wishes to know how much a lighting system for their football field will cost to operate. There are 4 poles each containing 16 fixtures of 1500 watts apiece, and 4 poles each containing 8 fixtures of 1650 watts apiece. If the school plans to use the lights about 120 hours per year, how much will it cost to run the lights at an average of 10 cents per kilowatt-hour?

When Are We Ever Gonna Have to Use This?

12. **Medical Lab Technician** (I)

Lab technicians use scientific notation to express the very large and very small numbers that arise constantly in lab work.

a. Red blood cells (RBC) are reported in RBC per cubic millimeter of blood. Normal value is about 5,000,000 RBC per cubic millimeter. Change this concentration to scientific notation.

b. Change 9700 WBC (white blood cells) per cubic millimeter to scientific notation.

13. **Technical Researcher** (II)

A detector in the Landsat satellite (see problem 10) produces 0.5 amperes of electrical current for each watt of reflected sunlight that falls on it. The detector gives a fluctuating current of 2×10^{-12} amperes without any sunlight. How many watts must fall on the detector to give a current 100 times greater than the fluctuating current?

Or Probability . . .

14. **Industrial Engineer** (III)

An engineer must have a die made for a plastic part. She has three choices of dies. The costs are outlined in the following chart:

Type of Die	Cost of Die	Unit Cost of Parts for an Order of:	
		Up to 10,000	10,000 or More
One Cavity	$3,000	$0.30 each	$0.25 each
Two Cavity	4,650	0.17 each	0.13 each
Three Cavity	5,800	0.11 each	0.09 each

The engineer is not certain how many parts she will need, but she estimates the probabilities as follows:

- There is a 0.2 probability she will need 3,000.

- There is a 0.5 probability she will need 12,000.

- There is a 0.3 probability she will need 20,000.

Which die should the engineer order? (**Hint:** First determine the cost for each amount with each die. Then, for each die, multiply the cost of each amount by its probability and add them together. Compare the totals for each die and pick the least expensive one.)

15. Technical Researcher (II)

A technical researcher is hired to do in-depth studies for various public and private agencies. For example, a law enforcement agency wanted to know the probability of a driver:

a. being intoxicated and having an accident

b. being unintoxicated and having an accident

c. being intoxicated, arrested, and convicted

d. being intoxicated, arrested, and dismissed

e. being intoxicated and having an unimpeded trip

The researcher discovered the following individual probabilities:

A driver being intoxicated	0.02

An intoxicated driver:
having an unimpeded trip	0.99911
having an accident	0.00045
being arrested	0.00044
having the case dismissed	0.30
being convicted after arrest	0.70

A driver not being intoxicated	0.98

An unintoxicated driver:
having an unimpeded trip	0.99984
having an accident	0.00016

Using these individual probabilities, find the combined probabilities asked for in (a) – (e) above. (A calculator is almost a must on this problem. Carry out answers as far as seven decimal places if necessary.)

Or Negative Numbers . . .

16. **Navigator** (I)

Low tide in port tomorrow is –0.7 feet. High tide is 16.9 feet. What is the tidal range?

17. **Printer** (I)

During the first ten days of the month, a printer recorded the following comparisons to the daily quota (+ means above quota, – means below quota): +$15.75, –$23.07, –$4.68, –$11.19, +$8.42, +$10.25, –$6.59, –$2.01, –$6.15, +$7.12. What was the overall total comparison to the quota?

Part 2: Practical Geometry

When Are We Ever Gonna Have to Use — Measurement and Conversion?

1. **Airplane Mechanic** (III)

    When riveting a piece of metal to an airplane, a mechanic must follow certain guidelines for the spacing of the rivets. For example, 1/4-inch rivets should be 1 1/4 inches apart. In addition, the first and last rivets should be 3/4 inch from the edge of the piece.

    As an example, to determine the number of rivets needed for a 4 1/2-foot section, first subtract 1 1/2 inches from 54 inches to account for the distance from each edge. This leaves 52 1/2 inches of length to be riveted. Next, divide this by 1 1/4 (the spacing between rivets) to get 42 spaces. Finally, add 1 to account for the fact that there is a rivet at each end of the interval. This means that 43 rivets are needed.

    Determine the number of 1/4-inch rivets needed for a piece of metal 5 feet 9 inches long.

2. **Auto Mechanic** * (II)

    An auto mechanic converts a metric part to 0.473 inch. The part comes only in fractional sizes given to the nearest 64th of an inch. What is the closest size?

3. **Construction Supplies Counter Clerk** (I)

    A customer orders 1200 pounds of rock. A small truck holds 3/4 ton. Will the truck be able to deliver the order?

4. **Construction Supplies Counter Clerk** (I)

    A customer wants to cement an area 8 feet by 16 feet by 4 inches deep. Since cement is measured in cubic yards, change each of these dimensions to yards.

5. **Contractor (General, Flooring)** * (II)

    Lumber is often measured in board feet. A board foot of lumber is a piece one foot square and one inch thick. To calculate board feet, multiply the thickness in inches by the width in feet by the length in feet. Count any thickness under one inch as one inch.

The floor of a small building requires 245 boards, each 2 inches thick by 12 inches wide by 12 feet long. How many board feet should be ordered?

6. **Dietician** (I)

The hospital dietician acts as the "middleman" between the doctor and the hospital cook. Sometimes the doctor will order food or liquid for a patient in one unit of measurement while the cook measures it using another unit. It is up to the dietician to convert the measurement.

If one ounce equals 30 grams, and a doctor orders 4 ounces of meat for a patient's dinner, how many grams should the cook be told to weigh?

7. **Dietician** (I)

A doctor orders 60 cc of juice for a certain patient's breakfast. If 120 cc is about 1/2 cup, how many cups of juice should the cook be told to measure?

8. **Dietician** (II)

If ordinary table salt is 40% sodium, and a doctor orders a diet containing 1 gram of salt, how many milligrams of sodium should the patient receive?

9. **Drafter (also Architect, Carpenter, Contractor)** (III)

Assuming that 1" by 6" redwood siding has a finished width of 5 1/2 inches, how many linear feet of siding are needed to cover a ceiling 15 feet 6 inches by 35 feet 3 inches? (Round the remainder up to the next whole number after each step.)

10. **Farm Advisor** (I)

Spray concentrations are often figured in metric measurement, especially when the amounts involve fractions of an ounce. For example, suppose a farmer needed 0.2367 ounces of active ingredient to deliver one pound per acre. Greater accuracy could be achieved by converting this to 7 milliliters and then measuring the amount.

Given that there are 29.57 milliliters in one fluid ounce, how many milliliters of active ingredient are equivalent to 1.606 ounces? (Round to the nearest 0.5 milliliter.)

11.   Hydrologist (III)

A hydrologist needs to know the number of gallons in an acre-foot. A conversion chart on flows tells her that 450 gallons per minute equals 2 acre-feet per 24 hours. From this information, compute the number of gallons in an acre-foot.

12.   Hydrologist (III)

If the flow into a reservoir is 15 cubic feet per second, how long (in hours, minutes, seconds) will it take to fill a 1,000,000-gallon reservoir? (**Hint:** 1 cubic foot = 7.48 gallons)

13.   Industrial Engineer (II)

A particular load exerts pressure of 26 pounds per square inch. How many pounds per square foot is this?

14.   Interior Decorator (II)

Ordering carpeting can be very complicated because it usually comes in 12-foot widths. If a customer had a 14-foot by 20-foot room to carpet, the decorator might design the following plan to minimize waste:

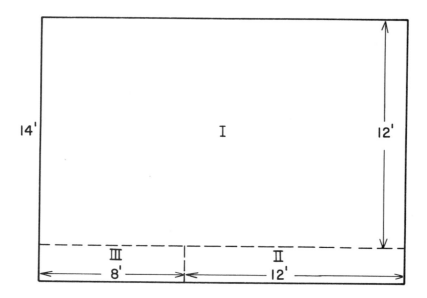

In this plan, Area I is 20 by 12 feet, Area II is 2 by 12 feet, and Area III is 2 by 8 feet. The only waste is a 2- by 4-foot section from Area III. The total amount needed is 24 by 12 feet.

There is a way to have no waste at all, but this would involve a large number of seams to patch the small pieces together, as shown below:

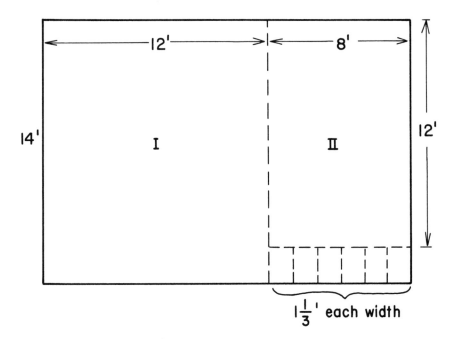

Design a way of carpeting each of the following room sizes using 12-foot widths of carpet. Waste as little as possible, but use no more than three seams.

a. 18 feet by 30 feet

b. 13 feet by 19 feet

15. Interior Decorator (II)

Ordering draperies can be complicated by the fact that many fabrics contain patterns. Lengthwise, the customer must purchase drapes in 1-foot increments. The excess must also be purchased if the required length falls in the middle of a pattern.

Suppose a customer needs 7-foot long drapes in a pattern that repeats lengthwise every 16 inches. What length must be purchased?

16. Interior Decorator (III)

Problem 15 explained how draperies are ordered in the length dimension. In the worked example below and the following problem, you will learn how widths are determined.

Suppose a customer wanted drapery for a window that is 100 inches wide. First you would need 13 additional inches for hems, overlap, and return. Next you would add "100% fullness" for pleats, giving you 226 inches. Finally, since this drapery only comes in 44-inch widths, you divide 44 into 226 and round up. (You cannot order a fraction of a width.) The final order would be 6 widths. Now try the following problem.

A window measures 92 inches wide. Allowing a total of 12 inches for return, overlap, and hems, how many widths of 54-inch wide drapery must be purchased? (Assume 100% fullness is needed.)

17. Marketing Representive (Computers) (I)

One of the jobs of a marketing rep is to help the customer fit the computer equipment into the available space. Since today's computer equipment comes in metric dimensions, the rep will often need to convert between English and metric units.

Will a machine 90 cm wide fit through a 3-foot wide doorway? (**Hint:** 1 inch = 2.54 cm)

18. Medical Lab Technician (I)

How many grams of NaCl (salt) would you add to a liter of water to make up a normal saline solution (0.85%, or 0.85 grams per 100 milliliters)?

19. Medical Lab Technician (II)

Many substances in a medical lab are now being measured in millimoles per liter, whereas they used to be given in milligrams per 100 milliliters. To convert the latter to the former, multiply mg/100 ml by 10 and divide by the molecular weight of the substance.

Convert a calcium solution of 12 mg/100 ml to millimoles per liter, given a molecular weight of 40.

20. Meteorologist (II)

If one inch of rain falls on an acre, how many tons of water fall?
(**Hint:** 1 cubic foot of water weighs 62.4 pounds, and 1 acre equals
43,560 square feet. Round to the nearest tenth.)

21. Motorcycle Sales and Repair (I)

Parts for Japanese motorcycles are metric. Sometimes a
customer will ask for a part for an American bike, and the
employee must convert to find the closest-sized metric part.

Suppose a customer needs a bolt 1/2 inch long and 1/4 inch in
diameter. Find the metric equivalents of these dimensions in
centimeters. (**Hint:** 1 inch = 2.54 cm)

22. Motorcycle Sales and Repair (I)

How many ounces of fork fluid are needed to fill a 190-cc tank?
(**Hint:** 1 ounce = 29.57 cc. Round to the nearest tenth.)

23. Nurse (III)

A pre-op solution must contain, among other ingredients, 0.2 mg
Atropine. The nurse has a solution of Atropine containing 0.8 mg
per cc. If 1 cc equals 16 minims, how many minims of the
solution will contain the required amount of Atropine?

24. Pharmacist (III)

Given that 1 cc weighs 1 gram in a particular case, how many
milligrams of neutral red does the pharmacist need to make 70 cc
of a 0.01% solution?

25. Photographer * (I)

The Mamiya RB 67 camera uses 120 film and produces 2 1/4-inch
by 2 3/4-inch negatives. How would this negative size be given in
millimeters in Japan? (**Hint:** 1 inch = 25.4 mm)

26. Plumber (County Inspector) (I)

Gas appliances are rated according to the number of BTU (British
Thermal Units) they require per hour. When designing gas
piping systems, plumbers must convert BTU per hour to cubic feet

of gas per hour. To the nearest cubic foot, how many cubic feet per hour are necessary to supply each of the following appliances? (**Hint:** There are 1100 BTU per cubic foot.)

a. Refrigerator: 3000 BTU

b. Range: 65,000 BTU

c. Furnace: 150,000 BTU

d. Water Heater: 50,000 BTU

27. **Plumber** (I)

If five sections of pipe measure 8 feet 6 inches, 6 feet 7 inches, 10 feet 4 inches, 9 feet 2 inches, and 4 feet 4 inches, what is the total length of pipe needed?

28. **Printer** (II)

A customer orders some brochures with 8 1/2- by 11-inch pages. The pages are printed on 17 1/2- by 22 1/2-inch sheets and then cut. How many of the larger sheets are needed for 8000 pages?

When Are We Ever Gonna Have to Use —
Area and Perimeter?

1. **Administrator (Shopping Mall)** (I)

   At $1.50 per square foot, determine the rent charged to the store occupying the area below:

   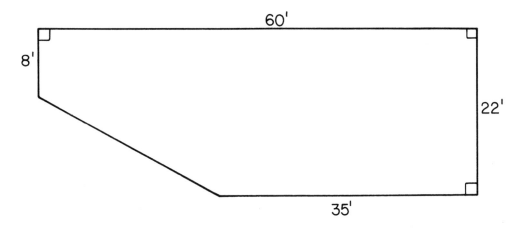

2. **Airplane Mechanic** (I)

   The area of a wing is equal to the span (S) times the average chord length (C).

   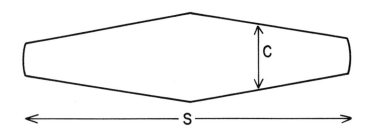

   Find the area of a wing whose span is 68 feet and whose average chord length is 7.5 feet.

3. **Appliance Store Manager** (II)

   The formula for determining the BTU (British Thermal Units) rating that is necessary for an air conditioner to cool a room is:

   BTU = Area (sq ft) × Exposure Factor × Climate Factor

   Use this formula to determine the BTU necessary to cool each of the rooms described in the chart on page 76.

Room Dimensions (ft)	Exposure Factor		Climate Factor	
22 by 16	North:	20	Buffalo:	1.05
13 by 12	West:	25	Portland:	0.95
17 by 14	East:	25	Topeka:	1.05
26 by 18	South:	30	San Diego:	1.00
23.5 by 15.3	North:	20	Tacoma:	0.95

4.   Architect (I)

The building code states that a particular building must have a minimum of 1250 square feet of yard, and that no dimension can be less than 20 feet. Would a yard be approved if it measured 32 ft by 38 ft? What about a 19-ft by 70-ft yard? A 42-ft by 35-ft yard?

5.   Attorney (II)

A client has inherited one-third of a piece of property. Since some parts of the 100-acre parcel are more valuable than others, the client is offered a 22-acre section planted in olive trees. From the legal description of the section offered, the attorney comes up with the sketch shown in the figure below. Determine whether or not it is equal to 22 acres. (**Hint:** There are 43,560 square feet in an acre.)

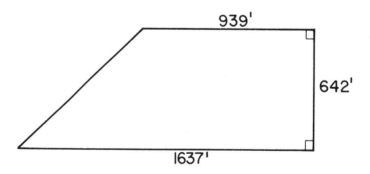

6.   Carpenter (I)

How many feet of form board material are needed to enclose a 4- by 6-foot concrete pad?

7.   Carpenter (I)

What length of hose do you need to put an air ring around a hot tub that is 6 feet in diameter? (Round up to the next whole foot.)

When Are We Ever Gonna Have to Use This?

8. Civil Engineer (III)

A fog seal must be applied to a 24-foot-wide roadway at the rate of 0.005 gallon per square yard. If there are 240 gallons of fog seal to the ton, how many tons are needed for 4.3 miles of road? (Round to the nearest hundredth.)

9. Civil Engineer (III)

The County Transportation Department must purchase some private land to put in a new right turn lane on an existing road. In the drawing, the dotted line represents the existing boundary, while the solid line represents the new right-of-way needed. Since the land is purchased by the acre, calculate the number of acres the county must purchase. (**Hint:** There are 43,560 square feet in an acre. Round to the nearest thousandth.)

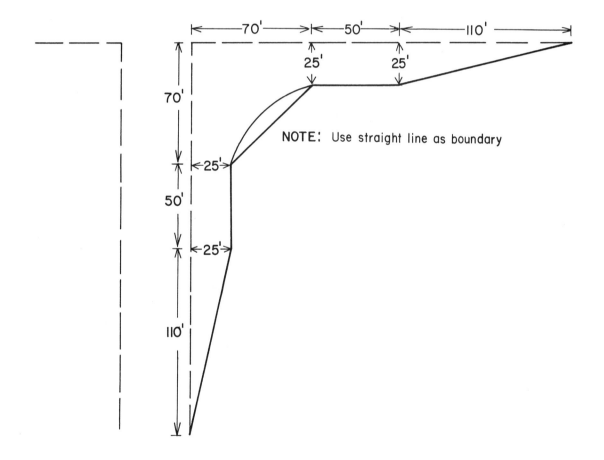

NOTE: Use straight line as boundary

10. **Construction Supplies Counter Clerk (also Masonry Contractor)** (II)

A certain type of brickwork requires about four bricks to the square foot. How many bricks are needed to make a path like the one in the figure below?

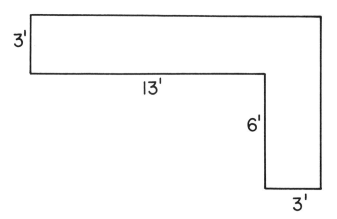

11. **Contractor (General)** (I)

A plastering contractor charges $16 per square yard. What is the cost for plastering 80 linear feet of wall in a house with a 9-foot ceiling?

12. **Flooring Contractor *** (I)

What is the cost of refinishing a wood floor in a room 35 feet by 20 feet at a cost of $2.50 per square foot?

13. **Forestry Land Management Planner** (III)

The path of a proposed oil pipeline will cross a total of 18.4 miles of National Forest land. The U.S. Forest Service charges the oil company a fee of $28 per acre for use of the land. The width of the land needed for the pipeline is 210 feet. Calculate the fee. (**Hint:** 1 mile = 5280 feet, and 1 acre = 43,560 sq ft)

14. **Forestry Recreation Management Officer** (II)

To find out how much use a recreational area is receiving, management officers need to compute the number of "visitor-hours" per day. Instead of sending people out to count visitors and their lengths of stay, the U.S. Forest Service has come up with an interesting way to estimate visitor-hours based on the area of a triangle.

Suppose a particular area had 126 cars in the parking lot at 2 P.M., the peak hour. Since the average number of visitors per car is 3.5 (a known statistic), then there were about 441 people in the park at that hour. If we assume that use of the park steadily increases from opening time (10 A.M.) to peak time, and then steadily decreases from peak time until closing, we can think of the daily use as a triangle:

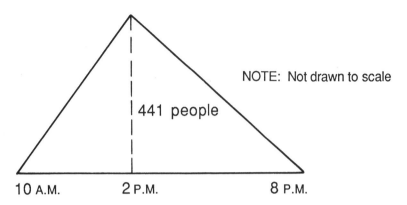

NOTE: Not drawn to scale

441 people

10 A.M.   2 P.M.   8 P.M.

The base of the triangle is 10 (the number of hours the park is open), and the height is 441 (the number of visitors during the peak hour). The area of the triangle, 2205, would be a reliable estimate of the number of visitor-hours per day.

Suppose a recreational area is open from 9 A.M. to 6 P.M. Forest Service data shows a daily average of 143 cars at the peak hour of 1 P.M. Assuming an average of 3.5 visitors per car, use the technique just explained to estimate the number of visitor-hours per day.

15.   Hydrologist (III)

One of the tasks of a hydrologist is to measure stream flow. The hydrologist uses this figure to determine such things as municipal water supply, flood control information, irrigation potential, and the oxygen supply for fish that inhabit the stream.

The stream flow, in cubic feet per second, is computed by multiplying the cross-sectional area of the stream (square feet) by the velocity of the water (feet per second). To determine the velocity of the water, the hydrologist may use a precise instrument such as a "pygmy meter," or the hydrologist may simply throw a twig in the stream and time how long it takes to travel a certain distance.

a. The cross-section of a particular stream approximates the shape of the trapezoid shown in the figure below. A hydrologist throws a twig in the stream and finds that it takes 7.5 seconds to travel 100 feet. Calculate the area of the trapezoid, the velocity of the stream in feet per second, and the stream flow in cubic feet per second.

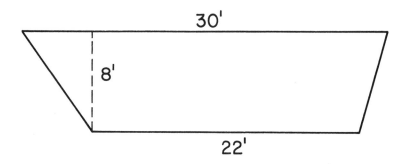

b. To gain a more accurate reading of the cross-sectional area of a stream, the hydrologist might take depth readings every 5 feet and compute the area of each resulting section as if it were a triangle or a trapezoid. Compute the cross-sectional area of the stream shown below. Then compute the flow of the stream if a pygmy meter showed a velocity of 2.5 feet per second.

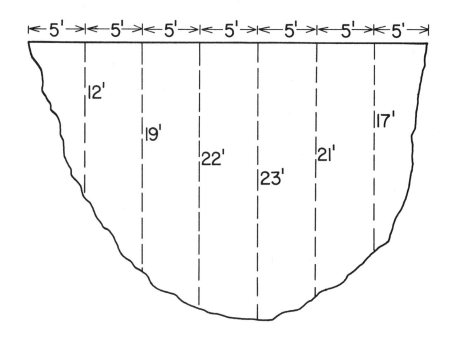

16. **Income Tax Specialist** (I)

Taxpayers who maintain an office in their home may deduct a percentage of their home-related expenses. This percentage is based on the area of their office compared to the area of their home.

The home of a client contains 2150 square feet. She maintains an office in the house that measures 13 feet by 9 feet.

a. What is the area of the office?

b. What percent of the area of her house does the office represent? (Round to the nearest tenth.)

17. **Industrial Engineer** (III)

Each production employee requires an average of 25 square feet of plant area. A blueprint of the plant is drawn to scale so that 1/32 of an inch equals 1 foot. How many employees will fit in an area that measures 18 1/2 inches by 7 1/8 inches on a blueprint?

18. **Insurance Agent** (III)

As rebuilding costs skyrocket, insurance agents must make sure their clients carry enough coverage on their home. At a rebuilding cost of $80 per square foot, how much coverage is needed for the house with the dimensions shown in the drawing below?

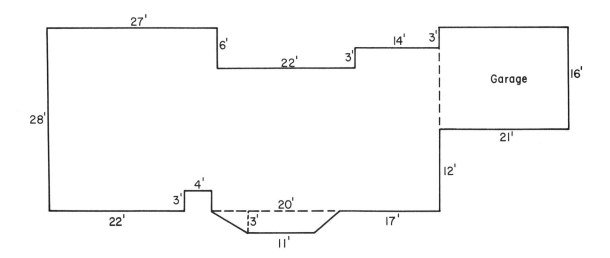

19. **Interior Decorator** (II)

A customer wants to surround a two-wall shower with synthetic marble to a height of 72". If the two walls measure 38" and 70" and marble costs $35 per square foot, what is the total cost of the marble?

20. **Interior Decorator** (II)

A room measures 24 feet by 16 feet.

a. How many square yards of carpeting are needed?

b. How many linear feet of tacking strip are needed for the perimeter?

21. **Landscape Architect** (III)

If asphalt pavement costs $0.78 per square foot, determine the cost of the circular road in the figure. Use 3.14 for pi and round to the nearest cent.

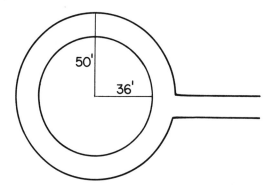

22. **Landscape Architect** * (I)

At $0.35 per square foot, how much will it cost to plant lawn sod in a square area that measures 14 feet 6 inches per side?

23. **Landscape Architect** (II)

How many plants spaced every 6 inches are needed to surround a circular walkway with a 25-foot radius?

When Are We Ever Gonna Have to Use This?

24. Machinist (III)

Find the bend length for the piece of metal shown in the figure below. Use the average of the inside and outside radius for your calculation and round to the nearest hundredth. (Assume that it is bent in a circular arc.)

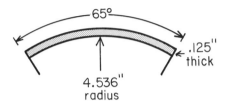

25. Machinist (I)

In a hexagon, the diagonal length is equal to twice the side length. What diameter of round stock must be used to cut a hex nut 1/4 inch on a side?

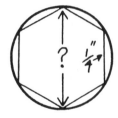

26. Machinist * (II)

If 8 bolts are to be spaced equally around a circular steel plate at a radius of 9 inches, what must be the spacing between the centers of the bolts along the curve?

27. Masonry Contractor (I)

The rule of thumb for blockwork is that 1.1 blocks are needed per square foot. How many blocks are needed for a wall 5 1/2 feet high and 87 feet long?

28. Meteorologist (III)

Meteorologists use a horizon circle of 360 degrees in computing and describing weather data. If a cloud mass 12 miles away from an observer obscures the horizon from 240 to 360 degrees, how wide is the cloud mass?

29. Painting Contractor (I)

One gallon of paint covers approximately 300 square feet. How much paint will you need to cover 340 feet of eaves with an average width of 4 feet?

30. Photographer (II)

A photographer has an amount of liquid formula that will tone the surface area of fifty 8" by 10" photographs. He needs to tone twenty-eight 11" by 14" photographs. Will he have enough?

31. Plumber (County Inspector) (II)

According to code, a certain rectangular duct in a restaurant must be 1.6 square feet in area. Because of structural limitations, the duct can only be 10 inches wide. How long must it be?

32. Printer (III)

A printer must run 5000 copies of a form printed on NCR paper (paper with a special type of carbon backing). An area 1 5/16 inches by 2 11/16 inches must be de-sensitized on each copy. If 1/2 pound of ink is needed per square inch to de-sensitize the paper, how many pounds of ink are needed for all 5000 copies? (Round to the nearest pound.)

33. Printer (III)

Some 5" by 7" photographs must be mounted on larger sheets to print. Mounting sheets come in 26" by 40" or 23" by 35" sizes. Determine the number of photographs that can be mounted on a sheet of each size. Then compute the amount of waste on each sheet as measured in square inches per photograph. (Assume that the photographs must be mounted consistently—that is, either all lengthwise or all widthwise.)

34. Real Estate Agent (II)

How many acres are in a piece of property measuring 1450 feet by 2185 feet? (**Hint:** There are 43,560 square feet in an acre. Round to the nearest tenth.)

When Are We Ever Gonna Have to Use This?

35. Real Estate Agent (II)

If each of the lots in the figure below measures 100 feet by 250 feet, what is the total square footage of the shaded region?

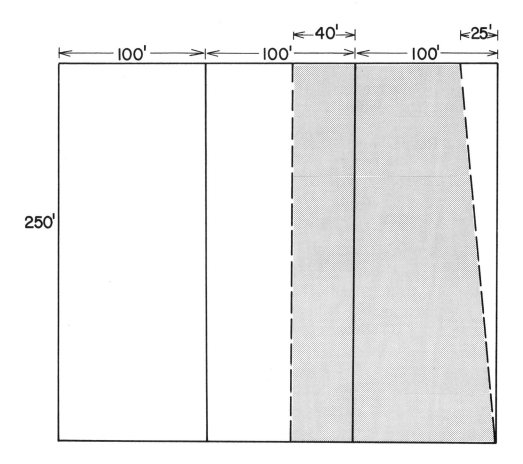

36. Real Estate Agent (I)

A realtor sold a rectangular lot with a 67.34-foot frontage and a 177.46-foot depth for $27.50 per square foot. What would be the total selling price? (Round to the nearest dollar.)

37. Sheet Metal, Heating, and Air Conditioning Specialist (II)

A 2-foot long section of pipe must be cut out of a 2-foot wide piece of sheet metal. The diameter of the pipe must be 8 inches with 1/2 inch extra for overlap. How long a piece of sheet metal must be cut to provide the necessary circumference? (Round to the nearest eighth-inch.)

38. **Sheet Metal, Heating, and Air Conditioning Specialist** (II)

A closed rectangular tank 60 inches by 20 inches by 10 inches must be covered inside with sheet copper lining. What is the total surface area to be covered?

39. **Sheet Metal, Heating, and Air Conditioning Specialist** * (II)

A rectangular opening 12" wide must have the same total area as two smaller vents measuring 6" by 4" and 8" by 5". What must be the height of the opening?

40. **Technical Researcher** (II)

The Landsat satellite circles the earth once every 100 minutes. The radius of the earth is 6370 km. How much ground will the satellite fly over in 30 seconds?

41. **Wastewater Treatment Operator** (II)

To find the hydraulic loading rate on a filter, divide the flow (in gallons per day) by the area of the filter (in square feet). Find the hydraulic loading rate on a circular filter 60 feet in diameter if the flow is 2,500,000 gallons per day. (Round to the nearest tenth.)

When Are We Ever Gonna Have to Use — Volume?

1. **Accountant** (II)

   An accountant for a small business must determine the amount of space needed on an ocean vessel to ship 2500 cylindrical drums that are each 2 feet 6 inches high and 15 inches in diameter. Find the total volume of the drums to the nearest cubic foot. Do not count space wasted between the drums.

2. **Airplane Mechanic** (I)

   How many cubic feet of baggage will a compartment 5 ft 6 in. by 3 ft 9 in. by 2 ft hold? Assume the shape is a rectangular prism.

3. **Attorney** (I)

   Your client, a contractor, is having a dispute with a property owner for whom the contractor installed a water tank. The owner does not believe that the tank holds the 500 gallons he was promised. The tank is in the shape of a cylinder. It has a radius of 3 feet and a height of 2 feet 4 inches. Given that there are about 7.5 gallons in a cubic foot, determine the number of gallons the tank holds.

4. **Civil Engineer** (III)

   How many cubic yards of concrete are needed to build a concrete pipe 9 feet long and 9 inches thick if the interior diameter must be 54 inches? (Round to the nearest hundredth.)

5. **Civil Engineer** (III)

   A trench 15 inches wide, 4 feet deep, and 160 feet long is dug for a metal pipe 6 inches in diameter. Assuming the pipe takes up the entire length of the trench, how many cubic yards of material are needed to backfill the trench? (Round to the nearest hundredth.)

6. **Civil Engineer** (III)

   A one-inch thick layer of asphalt concrete must be laid on a 24-foot wide roadway for 4.7 miles. If the material weighs 150 pounds per cubic foot, how many tons will be required?

7. **Civil Engineer** (II)

    If 0.24 sack of cement produces 1 cubic foot of concrete, how many sacks are needed for a 135-foot long retaining wall that has the cross-section shown in the figure below?

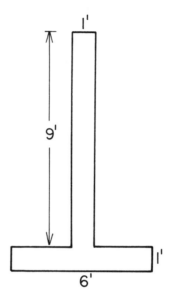

8. **Construction Supplies Counter Clerk** (III)

    A customer wishes to know the number of pounds of volcanic rock needed to fill an area 30 feet by 20 feet to a depth of 2 inches. If this type of rock weighs 1050 pounds per cubic yard, what do you tell the customer? (Round to the nearest pound.)

9. **Contractor** * (I)

    A pile of sand dumped by a hopper is cone-shaped. If the diameter of the base is 18 feet, and the height is 8 feet, how many cubic feet of sand are in the pile?

10. **Contractor (General or Heating)** (I)

    Will a furnace designed to heat 10,000 cubic feet be sufficient for a 1500-square-foot house with an 8-foot ceiling?

11. **Fire Fighter** (II)

    How many gallons of water would fill a 65-foot section of 2 1/2-inch diameter hose? (**Hint:** There are 231 cubic inches in a gallon. Round to the nearest tenth.)

When Are We Ever Gonna Have to Use <u>This</u>?

12.   Geologist (III)

The volume of water is often measured in acre-feet. One acre-foot of water would cover an acre to a depth of one foot.

Geologists may be hired to analyze groundwater wells. A particular groundwater reservoir has an area of 2500 acres, a thickness of 800 feet, and a specific yield of 10% (the actual percent of water that could be drawn from the reservoir). Use this information to answer the following questions.

a. How many acre-feet of water will the well yield?

b. Assuming a withdrawal rate of 1800 acre-feet per year, how long will the groundwater reservoir last?

13.   Hydrologist (II)

A large fire has denuded a hillside of vegetation. To gather flood control information, hydrologists drive nails into the soil prior to a large storm. (Assume the nailheads are flush with the soil surface.) After a storm an average of 1 1/4 inches of nail has been exposed over a rectangular area 260 feet by 475 feet. To the nearest hundred, how many cubic feet of soil were washed away?

14.   Industrial Engineer (III)

An engineer must design a tank that will hold 5000 gallons of water. If there are 7.48 gallons in a cubic foot, answer these questions to the nearest hundredth:

a. What diameter spherical tank will hold this amount?

b. How large a cube-shaped tank will hold this amount? (Give the edge length.)

15.   Landscape Architect (also Contractor) (II)

When grading a section of land, it is necessary to know the amount of dirt cut out of the higher elevation, and the volume needed to fill a lower elevation. These amounts of cut and fill should balance so that more dirt does not have to be brought in.

The landscape architect must compute the areas to be cut and filled, and then multiply each by the depth to arrive at the volume. The architect will usually assume a 10% loss of cut volume in determining whether there will be enough dirt for the fill.

Suppose that 8 feet of dirt must be removed from a 375-square-foot area and filled 4 feet deep into a 650-square-foot area. Allowing for a 10% loss of dirt from cut to fill, will there be enough to balance? How many loads will it take a truck with a capacity of 3 cubic yards to move the dirt?

16. **Machinist** * (II)

Find the weight of the cast iron shape shown below at 0.26 pounds per cubic inch. (Round to the nearest pound.)

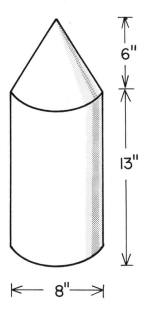

17. **Masonry Contractor** (II)

Building code dictates a 24" by 8" foundation for block walls. To the nearest tenth, how many cubic yards of concrete are needed for such a foundation if the wall is 120 feet long?

18. **Medical Lab Technician** (I)

A lab technician will often see an abnormal specimen under the microscope. In an effort to find out more about the specimen, the technician will calculate its volume.

Find the total volume of the cells marked with x's if each cell measures 0.1 mm by 0.1 mm and is 0.1 mm thick.

19. Motorcycle Sales and Repair (II)

The bore of a cylinder is its diameter, the stroke is its height, and the displacement is its volume. What is the displacement of a cylinder with a bore of 56.5 mm and a stroke of 49.5 mm? Give the answer in cubic centimeters.

20. Plumber (County Inspector) (III)

The top view of a septic tank 4 feet 3 inches deep is shown below. Use the figure to answer these questions:

a. What is the capacity in gallons? (1 cu ft = 7.48 gallons)

b. To what length would the 5-foot 9-inch dimension have to be stretched for a capacity of 1500 gallons?

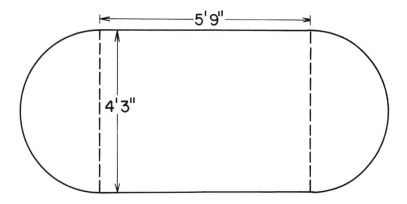

21. Plumber (County Inspector) (II)

A 6-inch diameter pipe 50 feet high is filled to the top with water. What is the weight at its base? (**Hint:** One cubic foot of water weighs 62.4 pounds. Round to the nearest pound.)

22. Plumber (County Inspector) (III)

In a 4-hour percolation test, 8 feet of water has seeped out of a cylindrical trench 4 feet in diameter. The code says that 5000 gallons must be absorbed by this particular trench in a 24-hour period. Given that there are 7.48 gallons in a cubic foot, will this soil pass the test?

23.   Printer (II)

How many boxes are needed to ship 8000 sheets of 8 1/2" by 11" paper, 0.005" thick, if each box measures 12" by 17" by 12"?

24.   Sheet Metal, Heating, and Air Conditioning Specialist (II)

A customer orders a 31-gallon tank to fit in a rectangular area measuring 14" by 8". How high should the tank be? (**Hint:** There are 231 cubic inches in a gallon. Round to the nearest inch.)

25.   Wastewater Treatment Operator (I)

A settling basin is 85 feet long, 24 feet wide, and 12 feet deep. How many gallons of water will it hold? (**Hint:** There are 7.48 gallons in a cubic foot.)

26.   Wastewater Treatment Operator (II)

How deep should a rectangular reservoir 50 feet long and 20 feet wide be in order to hold 400,000 gallons? (Round to the nearest tenth.)

27.   Wastewater Treatment Operator (II)

How many cubic feet of flow per day will pass through an open channel 5 feet wide and 1 foot deep if the velocity of water is 0.4 foot per second?

When Are We Ever Gonna Have to Use — The Pythagorean Theorem?

1. Forestry Land Management Planner (I)

Planners are considering construction of a road from a campsite directly to the entrance of a park (A to C in the diagram). Presently, they must travel 6 miles on one road, turn left, and travel 4 more miles on another road. Determine the length of the proposed road to the nearest tenth of a mile.

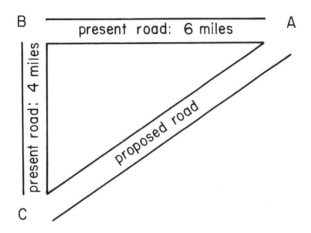

2. Industrial Engineer (III)

A magnetic head has worn down to the chord line AB measuring 0.250 inch. If the original gap depth is 0.125 inch, how much useful head life remains? (**Hint:** First solve for the current gap depth, X. Then subtract this from 0.125 inch.)

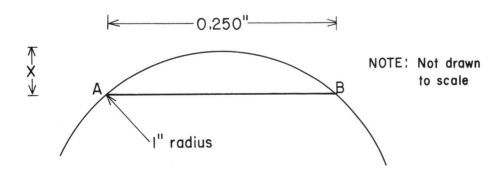

NOTE: Not drawn to scale

3. Meteorologist (also Airplane Pilot) (II)

An airplane pilot wishes to fly due east and reach a destination 200 miles away in 2 hours. If the wind is blowing from north to south at 20 mph, what air speed must the pilot maintain? (Round to the nearest mph.)

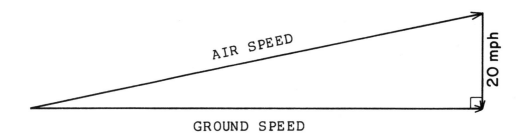

4. Meteorologist (III)

A weather balloon rises at the rate of 8 feet per second at a time when the wind is blowing at 9.44 miles per hour. After 15 minutes, how far away in feet from the launch point is the balloon? (Round to the nearest hundred feet.)

5. Photographer (I)

In choosing lenses a photographer sometimes will want to know the angle of view. This angle, α, is defined as illustrated:

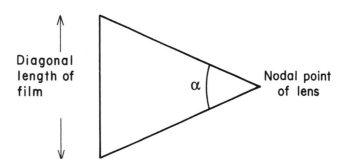

The first step in determining α is to calculate the diagonal length of the film. Given that 35-mm film is actually 36 mm by 24 mm, calculate the diagonal length of the film to the nearest tenth.

6. Plumber (County Inspector) (I)

A cold-water pipe must be offset 3 feet using 45-degree elbows. What is the length of the diagonal pipe to the nearest inch?

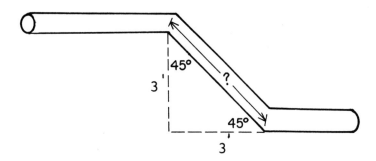

Part 3: Elementary Algebra

When Are We Ever Gonna Have to Use — Formulas?

1. **Accountant** (I)

    Accountants must determine whether a business is making enough profit. They use a figure called "gross profit percent," which is determined by the following formula:

    $$GP\% = \frac{\text{Sales} - \text{Overhead}}{\text{Sales}} \times 100$$

    Calculate the gross profit percent on sales of $850,000 and overhead of $550,000. (Round to the nearest tenth.)

2. **Airline Passenger Service Agent** (I)

    To determine the cost of shipping a live animal, airline personnel must first calculate the dimensional weight (D) of the kennel as given by

    $$D = \frac{LWH}{194}$$

    where L, W, and H are the dimensions of the kennel in inches. Find the dimensional weights of kennels having the following measurements:

    a. 30" by 24" by 18"

    b. 48" by 36" by 24"

    (Round to the nearest 0.1 lb)

    For added practice in calculating shipping cost, re-work problem 4 on page 35 using these results.

3. **Air Traffic Controller** (III)

    A pilot is having trouble with some of the airplane's navigation equipment and needs to know the distance to the airport.
    The pilot's aircraft is 90 degrees magnetic from the airport.

The control tower instructs the pilot to fly at a heading of 100 degrees. It takes the pilot 2 minutes 20 seconds to fly to this bearing. The aircraft's speed is 120 knots. Use the two formulas below to find the pilot's distance (in nautical miles) to the airport:

$$\text{Time to Airport (minutes)} = \frac{\text{Time (seconds) Between Bearings}}{\text{Degrees of Change}}$$

$$\text{Distance to Airport} = \frac{(\text{Speed}) \times (\text{Minutes to Airport})}{60}$$

4. **Auditor** (I)

Auditors are concerned with the "taxable measure" of a business when ownership is transferred. The formula is:

$$M = \frac{P(C + L)}{T}$$

M = taxable measure
P = taxable personal property
C = cash
L = liabilities assumed
T = total consideration

When a certain business was sold, $55,000 worth of taxable personal property changed hands. The buyer paid $6500 in cash, assumed $23,500 in liabilities, and gave the seller $45,000 in capital stock for a total consideration of $75,000. Compute the taxable measure of the business.

5. **Cartographer** (II)

Cartographers have discovered precise ways to determine what features and contours should be included on a map. The following formula gives the maximum length (S) for a line on a map. It is based on the original radius (R) of the curve being plotted and a constant known as the tolerance limit (E):

$$S = \sqrt{8RE - 4E^2}$$

Find the maximum length of a line if the original radius is 0.20 mm and the tolerance limit is 0.10 mm. (Round to the nearest hundredth.)

6. **Civil Engineer** (II)

The crushing load for a square pillar is given by the formula:

$$L = \frac{25T^4}{H^2}$$

L = crushing load (tons)
T = thickness of the wood (inches)
H = height of the post (feet)

Find the crushing load for a:

a. 4-inch thick post 8 feet high

b. 6-inch thick post 10 feet high

7. **Civil Engineer** (I)

A proposed road curves sharply as shown in the figure below. Use the formula

$$L = \frac{2\pi rm}{360}$$

to calculate the length (L) of the curve, given a radius (r) of 260 feet and a central angle measure (m) of 120°. (Round to the nearest 0.1 foot.)

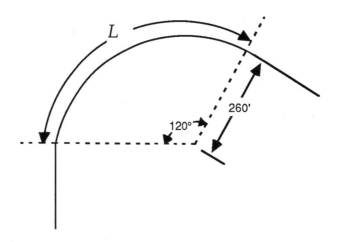

8. **Civil Engineer** (III)

When working with roadways, a civil engineer must use vertical curves. The drawing on page 99 shows a typical vertical curve. Definitions of the measurements are given below the drawing.

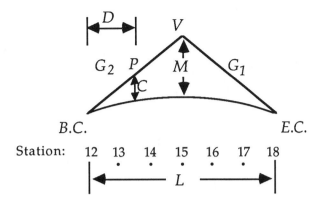

B.C. and *E.C.* represent the beginning of the curve and the end of the curve, respectively.

L is the length of the curve in 100-foot stations (*L* would be 6 in this example since the curve is 600 feet long).

G_1 and G_2 are the grade rates in percent.

V is the intersection of the grade lines.

M is the middle ordinate (vertical distance from *V* to the road).

D is the horizontal distance (in 100-foot stations) from *B.C.* or *E.C.* to the station referred to in the problem. Use the closer of the two distances.

C represents the correction from the grade line to the curve at that particular station.

Use the following formulas to solve problems (a), (b), and (c).

$$M = \frac{(G_2 - G_1)L}{8} \qquad C = \frac{4MD^2}{L^2}$$

a. The length of the curve is 600 feet, $G_1 = +3\%$, $G_2 = -2\%$. Find *M*, the middle ordinate.

b. Find *C*, the correction from grade line to curve, at station 14 ($D = 2$).

c. The result of part (b) is then added to the tangent elevation at the station to determine the actual elevation. If the tangent elevation at station 14 is 364.00 feet, find the actual elevation.

9. **Civil Engineer** (II)

In the figure below, a simple beam has a load that increases uniformly from one end to the other. The deflection (O_x) at some distance x from the end A is given by the following formula:

$$O_x = \frac{W}{180\ EIL^2}\ (3x^4 - 10L^2x^2 + 7L^4)$$

Find the deflection at a point 32 inches from A if $W = 5000$ lb, $E = 3 \times 10^7$, $I = 11.2$, and $L = 100$ inches. (Round to the nearest thousandth.)

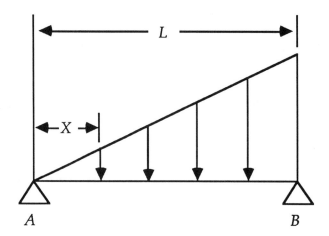

10. **Electrical Engineer** (I)

The capacity of a service using a 3-phase system is given by:

$$\text{Current} = \frac{P}{V\sqrt{3}} \qquad \begin{aligned} P &= \text{power (kilowatts)} \\ V &= \text{line voltage} \end{aligned}$$

Calculate the current (in amperes) for a 3-phase system in which there are 144 kw of power and 480 volts in the line. (Round to the nearest thousandth.)

11. **Electrical Engineer** (II)

Electrical engineers must design lighting systems that will provide enough light for the use of a room. They use the following formula to calculate the level of light in units called "foot-candles":

When Are We Ever Gonna Have to Use This?

$$F.C. = \frac{LDU}{A}$$

$$
\begin{aligned}
F.C. &= \text{foot-candles} \\
L &= \text{lumens} \\
A &= \text{area of room (square feet)} \\
D &= \text{coefficient of depreciation (light blocked by dirt, etc.)} \\
U &= \text{coefficient of utilization}
\end{aligned}
$$

Determine the foot-candle level for a 4-lamp fixture of 3100 lumens each in a room measuring 96 square feet. D equals 0.75 and U is 0.5 in this situation. (Round to the nearest tenth.)

12. Electrical Inspector (II)

The electrical service for a home must be sufficient to support the current needed. To compute the current in amperes, electricians use one of many commonly used formulas, such as:

$$I = \frac{P}{E}$$

$$
\begin{aligned}
I &= \text{current (amperes)} \\
P &= \text{power (watts)} \\
E &= \text{voltage}
\end{aligned}
$$

Compute the general lighting load in amperes for a single family dwelling of 1700 square feet if 3 watts are required per square foot. Assume a voltage of 115. (Round to the nearest tenth.)

13. Electrician * (I)

An electrician uses a bridge circuit to locate a ground in an underground cable several miles long. The following formula gives the distance to the ground:

$$x = \frac{R_2 L}{R_1 + R_2}$$

Find x if $R_1 = 750$ ohms, $R_2 = 250$ ohms, and $L = 4000$ ft.

14. Environmental Analyst (I)

When describing the environmental impact of a new commercial development, an analyst first considers the air pollutants contributed by the additional traffic. The formula for computing the number of pounds of pollutants per hour contributed by idling cars is:

$$P = \frac{TEC}{16}$$

T = number of trips
E = emission average
C = correction factor

Calculate the number of pounds of pollutants per hour of carbon monoxide for 1300 trips given an emission average of 0.0924 pound per mile and a correction factor of 0.29. (Round to the nearest hundredth.)

15. **Farm Advisor (or Civil Engineer)** (I)

Part of estimating the cost of grading an area of land is determining the amount of cut and fill that must be done. To approximate the volume of cut on a grid square, the following formula applies:

$$V = \frac{A(C + D + E + F)}{108}$$

V = volume of cut (cubic yards)
A = area of land (square feet)
C, D, E, F = depths of cut (feet) at the four corners

Calculate the approximate volume of cut for a 6400-square-foot area of land if the depths at the four corners are 2.3 ft, 0.6 ft, 1.4 ft, and 0.8 ft.

16. **Farm Advisor** (I)

The following formula gives the overall efficiency of a pumping plant:

$$E = PM$$

E = overall efficiency
P = efficiency of pump
M = efficiency of motor

Find the overall efficiency of a plant if the efficiency of the pump is 65% and the efficiency of the motor is 90%.

17. **Farm Advisor** (II)

The power required to pump one acre-foot of water in a year is given by:

$$KWH = \frac{1.024H}{E}$$

KWH = kilowatt hours
H = head, or total feet of lift
E = overall efficiency of plant

When Are We Ever Gonna Have to Use This?

Find the power required to pump 500 acre-feet of water per year given 150 feet of lift and an overall efficiency of 65%. (**Hint:** Be sure to change the percent to decimal form. Round to the nearest hundred.)

18.   Farm Advisor (I)

The size of the motor required for a pumping system can be found using the formula:

$$HP = \frac{DH}{3960E}$$

HP = horsepower of motor
D = pump discharge (gpm)
H = head (feet)
E = efficiency of pump

Compute the size of the motor required to pump 900 gpm (gallons per minute) given a 145-foot head and a pump efficiency of 62%. (Round to the nearest whole number.)

19.   Farm Advisor (I)

The following formula is used to determine the depth of water penetration in the soil while using stream irrigation:

$$D = \frac{RTP}{450A}$$

D = average penetration depth (in.)
R = rate of application (gpm)
T = time applied (hours)
P = soil penetration (in. per in.)
A = area of strip check (acres)

A half-acre strip check is irrigated for four hours at the rate of 400 gallons per minute. Find the average penetration depth if the soil penetration is 5 inches per inch of water applied. (Round to the nearest inch.)

20.   Fire Fighter (I)

The velocity (feet per second) of water discharged from a nozzle is given by:

$$V = 12.14 \sqrt{P} \qquad P = \text{pressure at the nozzle}$$

Find the velocity of discharge if the nozzle pressure is 65 psi. (Round to the nearest whole number.)

21.   **Fire Fighter** (II)

The flow rate (Q) of water in gallons per minute is given by:

$$Q = 29.7D^2 \sqrt{P}$$

D = diameter of the nozzle
P = static pressure (psi)

Calculate the flow of water from a 1 1/4" nozzle at 50 psi. (Round to the nearest gpm.)

22.   **Fire Fighter** (II)

The friction loss (FL) in psi per 100 feet for a 2 1/2" hose is found using:

$$FL = 2Q^2 + Q$$

Q = the flow rate in 100 gpm

What would the friction loss be in a 275-foot line of 2 1/2" hose discharging 350 gpm? (**Hint:** Be careful of units. The flow rate and the friction loss are both in hundreds.)

23.   **Fire Fighter** (II)

The maximum horizontal range (S) of a fire stream is calculated using the formula:

$$S = 0.5N + 26$$

S is in feet and N is the nozzle pressure in pounds for a 3/4" nozzle. Add 5 feet to the answer for every 1/8" increase in nozzle diameter over this.

The nozzle pressure is 86 pounds and the nozzle diameter is 1 3/8". What is the maximum horizontal range of the stream?

24.   **Fire Prevention Officer** (II)

Forestry officials have developed a formula for determining the damage potential to a particular area in case of a fire. This figure is then used to decide the best allocation of the fire prevention budget. The formula is:

$$D = 2A + V$$

D = damage potential
A = average brush age
V = value class (the higher the number, the greater the value)

Rank the following areas in order of damage potential:

	Average Brush Age	Value Class
Area 1	1 year	6
Area 2	10 years	3
Area 3	5 years	7

25. Forestry Land Management Planner (III)

In planning, decisions are made by comparing costs to benefits. But when planners are going to spend or earn money in the future, the money is worth less than if it were spent or earned now because of the interest it could be earning in the meantime. The following formula discounts all future money to present-day value:

$$V_o = \frac{V_n}{(1 + p)^n}$$

V_o = present-day value
V_n = value n years from now
n = years from now money is spent
p = interest on \$1 for 1 year

Forestry planners are trying to find the benefit-to-cost ratio of a fuel break. The total costs are \$165,000 and include such items as brush clearing, timber loss, and wildlife and watershed impact. Of this total, \$45,000 would be spent 1 year from now, \$90,000 would be spent 2 years from now, and \$30,000 would be spent 4 years from now. The benefits, namely the avoidance of damage and fire fighting expenses, would be \$6,500,000 (10,000 acres at \$250 per acre for fire fighting and \$400 per acre for damage) realized 10 years from now.

Using the formula, discount each of the three costs and the one benefit to present-day value. Assume a 10% interest rate (\$0.10 on \$1 for 1 year) and compute the overall benefit-to-cost ratio to the nearest tenth.

26. Income Tax Specialist (II)

A large tax preparation business runs a school for new tax preparers just prior to the busy season. Two formulas are used for estimating the proper number of new students to enroll to ensure that there are enough preparers:

$$Q = \frac{PV_L}{P + V_L} \qquad \text{or} \qquad Q = 4(3V_P - R)$$

P = population in thousands
V_L = last year's volume in thousands
V_P = projected volume in ten-thousands
R = number of returning preparers

Use both formulas to come up with estimates of a student quota given:

- a projected volume of $220,000
- $205,000 volume last year
- a population of 80,000
- 50 returning preparers

27. Industrial Engineer (II)

In pushing a load up a slope, the force required (discounting friction) is given by:

$$F = LS \qquad \begin{aligned} F &= \text{the force in pounds} \\ L &= \text{the load in pounds} \\ S &= \text{the slope (decimal)} \end{aligned}$$

Find the force required to drive a 15,000-lb load up a slope that rises 1/4" in 10 ft.

28. Industrial Engineer (II)

A fluid pump must be designed to pump 41 quarts of liquid per minute. The speed of the pump is 6857 rpm. The displaced area (area that the liquid covers while in the pump) is 0.65 in.^{2} Determine the length of the pump using the formula:

$$\text{Length (in.)} = \frac{\text{Flow rate (gal/min)} \times 231 \text{ (in.}^3\text{/gal)}}{\text{speed (rpm)} \times \text{displaced area (in.}^2\text{)}}$$

(Round to four decimal places.)

29. Insurance Claims Supervisor (also Highway Patrol Officer) (I)

Claims adjusters and highway patrol officers are concerned with establishing who was at fault in an accident. To help them find the cause, they use skid marks to determine the speed of the vehicles. They may use either a graph (see page 55) or the formula below to find the speed based on a straight skid:

$$V = \sqrt{30FS}$$

V = the velocity (mph)
F = the coefficient of friction of the road (changed to a decimal)
S = the skid length (feet)

Use this formula to compute the velocity of a car skidding 225 feet on a roadway with a 40% coefficient of friction. (Round to the nearest mph.)

30. Insurance Claims Supervisor (also Highway Patrol Officer) (III)

In Problem 29 you found the speed of a vehicle that leaves a straight skid. Sometimes a vehicle will leave circular or centrifugal skid marks. To find the speed in this case, two formulas are used. The first formula below will find the radius of the skid, while the second formula will find the actual speed of the vehicle.

$$R = \frac{3C^2}{2M} + \frac{M}{24} \qquad\qquad V = \sqrt{15RF}$$

R = radius of skid (inches)
C = chord length (feet)
M = mid-ordinate (inches)
V = velocity (mph)
F = coefficient of friction (changed to decimal)

A road surface has a 60% coefficient of friction. Find the speed of a car leaving a centrifugal skid with a chord length of 45 feet and a mid-ordinate of 13 inches. (Round to the nearest mph.)

31. Insurance Claims Supervisor (also Highway Patrol Officer) (I)

In unusual situations the coefficient of friction of the road will be unknown. To determine the coefficient, the following formula is used:

$$F = \frac{V^2}{30S}$$

F = coefficient of friction
V = velocity of test vehicle (mph)
S = skid length of test vehicle (ft)

Determine the coefficient of friction of a road surface on which a car traveling 55 mph skids to a stop after 320 feet. (Round to the nearest hundredth.)

32. Landscape Architect (also Farm Advisor) (I)

In designing a sprinkler system that will water all areas thoroughly, a landscape architect must calculate the "precipitation rate" (PR) of the system in inches per hour as given by the formula:

$$PR = \frac{96.3F}{SL}$$

F = flow in gallons per minute
S = spacing between sprinklers (ft)
L = spacing between rows (ft)

Calculate the precipitation rate for a sprinkler system applying 80 gpm with 20 feet between sprinklers and 15 feet between rows.

33. Landscape Architect (also Civil Engineer) (II)

When grading land for a road, it is important to know the slope of the road. The following formula is used:

$$S = \frac{D}{L}$$

S = the slope
D = the difference in elevation
L = the horizontal length

On an architectural drawing of a roadway, point A has an elevation of 83.2 feet, and point B is at 86.7 feet. The distance between the two points is 50 feet. Find the slope between the two points in the form of a percent.

34. Machinist * (I)

To find the taper per inch of a piece of work, a machinist uses the following formula:

$$T = \frac{D - d}{L}$$

D = diameter of the large end
d = diameter of the small end
L = length

Find T if D = 4.1625 inches, d = 3.2513 inches, and L = 8 inches.

35. Machinist * (I)

Machinists use an equation known as Pomeroy's formula to determine approximately the power required by a metal punch machine.

$$P = \frac{t^2 dN}{3.78}$$

P = power needed (in horsepower)
t = thickness of the metal
d = diameter of the hole to be punched
N = number of holes punched at once

Find the power needed to punch six 2"-diameter holes at once in a sheet 1/8" thick. (Round to the nearest hundredth.)

36. Machinist (I)

Hexagonal shapes are often cut from round stock. Many times the machinist will know the distance between the "flats" (f). He will then need to find the distance between the corners (d) in order to know the diameter of round stock to use.

Use the formula d = 1.1547f to find the diameter of round stock needed to cut a hex nut measuring 1.3750" between the flats. (Round to the nearest ten-thousandth.)

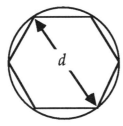
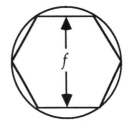

37. Medical Lab Technician (II)

The concentration of an enzyme is given by:

$$C = \frac{A V_T}{f V_S}$$

A = absorbance as read on a spectrometer
V_T = total volume
V_S = sample volume
f = a constant for the substance

Find C in scientific notation if A = 0.285, V_T = 3.1, V_S = 0.1, and f = 6.22×10^3.

38. Oceanographer (Biological) (II)

Oceanographers use a quantity known as shoreline development to describe and categorize bodies of water. Shoreline development (D) measures how closely a body of water resembles a circle, and it is given by the formula:

$$D = \frac{L}{2\sqrt{\pi A}}$$

L = the length of the shoreline
A = the area of the body of water
(In a perfect circle, $D = 1$.)

Find D for a lake with an area of 1,542,600 square meters and a shoreline length of 5600 meters. (Round to the nearest hundredth.)

39. Petroleum Engineer (III)

This problem will determine the total amount of recoverable gas reserves in a natural reservoir. The data gathered by the engineers is as follows:

Rock porosity	=	R	= 22%	= 0.22
Water saturation	=	S	= 23%	= 0.23
Reservoir area	=	A	= 160 acres	
Reservoir thickness	=	H	= 40 ft	
Initial pressure	=	I	= 3250 psia	
Temperature	=	T	= 673° F	
Final pressure	=	F	= 500 psia	
Gas compressibility at I	=	Z	= 0.91	
Gas compressibility at F	=	Y	= 0.951	

The formula for determining the recoverable volume of gas is:

$$V_R = V_i - V_L$$

V_R = recoverable gas reserves
V_i = initial gas volume in place
V_L = gas left in place at 500 psia

The formulas for V_i and V_L are:

$$V_i = \underbrace{(43{,}560\,AH)}_{\substack{\text{rock} \\ \text{volume}}} \times \underbrace{R\,(1 - S)}_{\substack{\text{space con-} \\ \text{taining gas}}} \times \underbrace{\left(\frac{520°}{T} \times \frac{I}{14.65} \times \frac{1}{Z} \right)}_{\substack{\text{conversion to} \\ \text{standard pressure} \\ \text{and temperature}}}$$

For V_L use the above formula, substituting F for I and Y for Z.

Use the data and the formulas to find V_R, the volume of recoverable gas reserves. (Express your answer in scientific notation, and round to the nearest thousandth.)

40.   Photographer (I)

To shoot a close-up exposure, you must increase the distance between the lens and the film in order to focus. The effective *f*-stop is altered by this, and the numbers on the barrel of the lens no longer apply. You must use the following formula to determine the increase in exposure (*f*-stop):

$$\text{Exposure Factor} = \frac{\text{Focal Length + Extension}}{\text{Focal Length}}$$

Find the necessary increase in the *f*-stop if the focal length is 80 mm and the extension is 40 mm.

41.   Purchasing Agent (II)

The following formula has been developed for purchasing agents to determine the optimum quantity in which to order an item:

$$EOQ = \sqrt{\frac{2rs}{pi}}$$

EOQ = order quantity (units)
r = annual requirement of the item
s = purchase cost per order
p = price paid per unit
i = annual inventory carrying charge as a percent of average inventory value

Find the optimum order quantity of safety caps given: 500-unit annual requirement; purchase cost of $1 per order; unit price of $0.89; annual inventory carrying charge of 18% (0.18).

Note: In determining the ability of a solar heating system to meet the energy needs of a household, a heating specialist would begin with problem 36 on page 17 and then work problems 42–45 below. To understand the entire process, all five problems should be worked in order.

42.   Sheet Metal, Heating, and Air Conditioning Specialist (I)

Problem 36 on page 17 involved computing the "coefficient of heat transfer" for the walls of a house. This figure is used as part of the following formula to calculate Q, the number of BTU per hour needed from a heating system to maintain the temperature at a particular level:

$$Q = UAD$$

U = the coefficient of heat transfer for a particular surface
A = the area of that surface in square feet
D = the difference in temperature between the desired reading and the lowest outside temperature

Suppose the wall area of a house is 1518.5 sq ft, and U = 0.0679. Find the wall component of Q if the desired temperature is 70° and the lowest outside temperature is 30°. (Round to the nearest hundred.)

43.   Sheet Metal, Heating, and Air Conditioning Specialist (I)

After calculating Q, the total BTU per hour for all surfaces for a heating system (see problem 42), the heating specialist next determines the number of BTU per month (M) using the following formula:

$$M = \frac{24 \times Q \times DDM}{D}$$

DDM = the number of degree days per month of heater use
D = the degree difference between the inside goal and the outside minimum

Find M if D = 40°, DDM = 545, and the total value of Q is 28,600 BTU/hour.

44. Sheet Metal, Heating, and Air Conditioning Specialist (I)

The next formula is used to calculate the BTU per month for heating the hot water for a house:

$$H = N \times GPD \times 8.33 \times D$$

N = the number of days in the month
GPD = the gallons per day of hot water use
8.33 = the weight in pounds of a gallon of water
D = the difference in temperature between heated water and tap water

Calculate H for a 31-day month if the residents use 50 gallons per day, and the difference between heated water and tap water is 80°.

45. Sheet Metal, Heating, and Air Conditioning Specialist (II)

After computing the total energy need for all 12 months, the next step in evaluating a solar system is to find the total energy produced by the system. The formula for any particular month is:

$$S = IEPNA$$

I = the amount of sunlight energy per square foot
E = the efficiency rating of the solar panels
P = the percent of sunshine on an average day
N = the number of days in the month
A = the area in square feet of the panels in the system

a. A solar heating system contains 180 sq ft of panels rated at 58% efficiency. Find S for a 31-day month in which the sun shines 68% of the time at an energy level of 2118 BTU per square foot. (Change the percents to decimals.)

b. Suppose the total heating need for this household was 5.84×10^7 BTU/year, and the total energy supplied by the solar heating system was 4.42×10^7 BTU/year. Compute the percent of the total need that the solar system provides.

46. Sheet Metal, Heating, and Air Conditioning Specialist * (II)

To make a right-angle inside bend in sheet metal, the length of sheet used is given by the following formula:

$$L = x + y + \frac{T}{2}$$

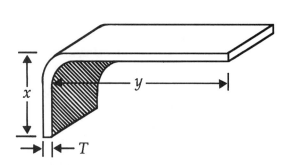

Find L when $x = 6\,1/4"$, $y = 11\,7/8"$, and $T = 1/4"$.

47. Technical Researcher (I)

In designing a rapid transit system, researchers have devised the formula $r = 0.334V^2$ to describe the minimum radius of a curve (in feet) that would ensure passenger comfort. V stands for the velocity of the vehicle.

Find the minimum radius of a curve for a velocity of 50 mph.

48. Television Repair Technician (I)

One of the forms of Ohm's Law, $I = E/R$, is often used in television repair. Find the current (I, given in amperes) in a circuit if the voltage (E) measures 100 volts across a 5-ohm (R) resistor.

49. Television Repair Technician (II)

The formula $P = E/I$ is used to find the power (P) in watts given a voltage (E) and a current (I) in amperes. Allowing a 20% leeway, how high a wattage rating should a resistor have for a 100-volt circuit with a current of 20 amps?

50. Temporary Employment Agency Clerk (III)

The manager of an employment agency has devised the formula

$$GP = N - (F + T + P)$$

to determine gross profit (GP) in terms of net sales (N), franchise fee (F), temporary employee wages (T), and payroll taxes (P).

a. Since the franchise fee is 3% of net sales ($F = 0.03N$) and the payroll taxes are 14% of the temporary employee wages ($P = 0.14T$), substitute these values in the original formula to restate GP in terms of N and T only.

b. Find the gross profit if net sales were $2932.50 and temporary employee wages were $1955.

51. **Temporary Employment Agency Clerk** (II)

Because it is part of a franchise, the employment agency must pay a fee to the national office. The fee is a percentage of either its sales or its gross profit. Since the manager has her choice, she will naturally want to pay whichever fee is lower. Unfortunately, one fee is not always lower than the other because the profit percent varies. Because of her background in algebra, the manager was able to devise a formula that would tell her the billing rate (x) at which the two fees were the same. At any rate higher than x the fee based on sales is lower, and at any rate lower than x the fee based on gross profit is lower.

$$x = \frac{F_G(r + p)}{F_G - F_S}$$

F_G = the fee based on gross profit
r = the pay rate to employees
p = the payroll tax
F_S = the fee based on sales

a. Find x if F_S is 0.03, F_G is 0.12, r is $7.50, and p is 0.14.

b. Based on your answer to (a), which fee should the manager choose if the billing rate is $8.38?

52. **Wastewater Treatment Operator** (I)

The formula for finding the amount of chlorine to add to a basin is:

$A = 8.34FC$

A = the amount of chlorine in pounds
F = the flow in millions of gallons per day (MGD)
C = the desired concentration of chlorine in parts per million (ppm)

Determine the amount of chlorine to add if the flow is 8 MGD and the desired concentration is 30 ppm.

53. Wastewater Treatment Operator (I)

The formula for detention time (the amount of time water remains in a tank) is given by:

$$T = \frac{V}{Q}$$

T = detention time in days
V = volume of the tank in gallons
Q = flow rate in gallons per day

Find the detention time of a tank holding 22 million gallons with a flow rate of 1.5 million gallons per day. (Round to the nearest tenth.)

When Are We Ever Gonna Have to Use — Linear Equations?

1. Accountant (II)

As shown in problem 1 on page 96, an accountant uses the following formula to find gross profit percent:

$$GP\% = \frac{Sales - Overhead}{Sales} \times 100$$

Suppose the company wanted to make a gross profit of 25% on sales of $1,500,000. What would be the maximum possible overhead?

2. Auto Mechanic (II)

An independent auto mechanic, like many other business owners, may be responsible for doing the bookkeeping. Sometimes a situation occurs in which the mechanic knows the total figure for parts, including the tax, and the sales tax needs to be separated from the cost of the parts.

Assuming a sales tax of 6%, write an equation that will allow you to solve for the cost (P) of the parts on a total bill of $14.71. Then solve the equation and subtract to find the tax.

3. Civil Engineer (II)

A concrete mix is in volume proportions of 1 part cement, 2 parts water, 2 parts aggregate, and 3 parts sand. How many cubic feet of each ingredient are needed to make 1 cubic yard of concrete? (**Hint:** Write an equation and then solve it, using the fact that 1 cu yd = 27 cu ft.)

4. Civil Engineer (II)

A tunnel is being dug under a mountain beginning at one end at an elevation of 645 feet above sea level. The tunnel will be constructed at a constant upward slope of 6%.

a. Write an equation for y, the elevation of the tunnel, in terms of x, the horizontal distance from the start.

b. Find the elevation of the tunnel 3800 feet from the starting point.

5.   Civil Engineer (II)

An engineer estimates the costs of constructing a roadway as follows: The pavement will cost twice the amount of the base material, and the sidewalk will cost one-fourth the amount of the pavement. Calculate the cost of each item on a $280,000 road project.

6.   Civil Engineer (II)

Steel tapes used in surveying are 100.00 ft long at 68° F. The tapes expand at a rate of 0.00000645 foot per foot of tape per degree of temperature increase. They also contract at the same rate. Find the actual distance between two points if the measured distance is:

a. 503.25 ft at 105° F.

b. 1134.75 ft at 48° F.

(Round to the nearest hundredth.)

7.   Electrical Engineer (II)

In problem 11 on pages 100-101, the following formula was given to find the foot-candle level of light in a room:

$$F.C. = \frac{LDU}{A}$$

L = lumens
A = area of room (square feet)
D = coefficient of depreciation
U = coefficient of utilization

Use this formula to solve for the number of lumens necessary to provide 80 foot-candles of light in a 9- by 14-foot room. Use $D = 0.8$ and $U = 0.6$.

8.   Electrical Engineer (II)

When you draw current from a generator or battery, the original voltage begins to drop. The formula $V = E - IR$ gives the new voltage (V) based on the original voltage (E), the current (I), and the resistance (R). For troubleshooting purposes, an engineer may wish to find the current after measuring the voltage.

Suppose a battery had a starting voltage (E) of 28 V. As current was being drawn, the voltage dropped to 25 V. Find the amount of current drawn (in amperes) if the resistance is 0.05 ohms.

9. **Electrical Engineer** (III)

A wheel containing optical devices is located at the back of a telescope. A motor causes the wheel to move to various positions and stop, depending on which device is to be used. In order to do its job, the motor must accelerate the wheel through a 30° angle (0.52 radian) in 0.05 second from a standing start. The inertia of the wheel is 0.04 in. oz sec²/rad. Assuming a constant acceleration, how much torque must the motor develop? Use the following formulas:

$$x = 0.5at^2 \qquad\qquad T = aI$$

x = the angle position in radians
a = the acceleration
t = time
T = torque
I = inertia

(**Hint:** First solve the first equation for a. Then calculate a with the given data. Finally, substitute a and the given value of I into the second equation.)

10. **Electrician** (I)

The classic form of Ohm's Law that every electrician learns is $I = E/R$, where I is the current in amperes, E is the electromotive force in volts, and R is the resistance in ohms. Since there are many cases in which E and R must be found, the electrician must also be able to convert the equation to two other forms.

a. Solve Ohm's Law for E and for R.

b. Find the voltage necessary to push a 0.5-amp current through a resistance of 440 ohms.

c. What is the resistance of a motor drawing 90 amps from a 6-volt battery? (Round to the nearest hundredth.)

11. **Farm Advisor** (I)

Problem 19 on page 103 illustrates the use of the following formula to find D, the average penetration depth in inches during stream irrigation:

$$D = \frac{RTP}{450A}$$

R = rate of application (gpm)
T = time applied (hours)
P = soil penetration (in. per in.)
A = area of strip (acres)

You can also use this formula to solve for T when you know D, R, P, and A.

A farmer wishes to achieve a penetration depth of 30 inches in soil that allows 9 inches of penetration per inch of water applied. How many hours must a one-half acre strip of soil be watered at a rate of 450 gallons per minute?

12. **Hydrologist** (III)

Stream C, running at 12 cu ft/sec, is fed by two other streams, A and B. Stream A contributes 4 cu ft/sec and stream B adds 8 cu ft/sec. The dissolved oxygen is 4% in stream A and 6% in stream B.

a. How much dissolved oxygen is available in stream C?

b. Fish living in stream C need 5.5% dissolved oxygen in order to survive. Several steps can be taken to increase the present amount. For example, the water can be aerated by adding water with a high percentage of dissolved oxygen. Another alternative is to reduce the pollutants that rob the stream of oxygen.

Suppose an industrial plant located on stream A was adding pollutants to the water. What level of dissolved oxygen would have to be achieved in stream A in order to increase the dissolved oxygen in stream C to the desired level of 5.5%?

13. **Income Tax Specialist** (III)

Under the Keogh money purchase pension plan, self-employed individuals may contribute up to 25% of their *earned income* tax-free to their plan. Earned income is defined as net income minus the actual contribution.

a. What percent of *net income* does the maximum allowance actually amount to?

b. If an accountant's net income is $33,000, how much may she contribute to the plan?

14.   Medical Lab Technician (I)

There are many standard formulas used in lab work. One example is:

$$Hct = \frac{RC \times MCV}{10}$$

$$
\begin{aligned}
Hct &= \text{the ratio of liquid to solid in blood} \\
RC &= \text{the red cell count} \\
MCV &= \text{mean cell volume}
\end{aligned}
$$

In order to determine the type of anemia a sample indicated, the lab technician needs to solve for the mean cell volume. Find *MCV* in terms of the other variables in the formula.

15.   Navigator (I)

In navigation, the distance-rate-time formula $D = RT$ is the most common one used.

a. Solve for R and for T in terms of the other variables. Since it may be necessary to solve for rate or time, it is important to know these two variations of the formula.

b. What average speed (in knots) has a ship maintained if it covered 48 miles in 3 hours and 12 minutes?

c. How long will it take to cover a distance of 31 miles given a cruising speed of 9 knots? (Round to the nearest minute.)

16.   Petroleum Engineer (III)

A spherical tank 60 ft in diameter must be designed to store gas. It is constructed from steel that can withstand 30,000 psi (pounds per square inch). The working pressure of gas is 75 psi. The following formulas apply:

$$P = p\pi r^2$$

$$
\begin{aligned}
P &= \text{force exerted by the gas (lb)} \\
p &= \text{pressure of the gas (psi)} \\
r &= \text{radius of the sphere (in.)}
\end{aligned}
$$

$$F = 2\pi rst$$

F	= reactive force from the steel (lb)
s	= strength of the steel (psi)
t	= thickness of the steel (in.)
r	= radius of the sphere (in.)

Find the minimum thickness of the steel given that, at the minimum, the force of the gas is equal to the reactive force from the steel.

17. **Pharmacist** (II)

How many cc of water should be added to 25 cc of a 95% acid solution to dilute it to a 50% solution?

18. **Pharmacist** (I)

Some quantities, such as glycerine, are often ordered in volumetric units but are measured in terms of weight. If glycerine has a density of 1.25 g/cc, find the weight in grams for a 45-cc order of glycerine by solving the following formula:

$$\text{Volume} = \frac{\text{Weight}}{\text{Density}}$$

19. **Political Campaign Manager** (II)

A political campaign manager in a small town must decide whether to purchase a bulk-rate permit for mailing campaign literature. The permit costs $50, and the bulk mailing rate is 16.7 cents per piece. If first-class postage is 25 cents per piece, how many pieces would have to be mailed to make the bulk rate more economical than first class?

20. **Publishing House Production Manager** (III)

Equations are often used to determine the selling price of a book. Here is a worked example of how to build this equation, followed by a problem for you to solve.

The manufacturing cost of a book is $5.65.

The average percent of author royalties is 11.5% of the selling price. If x represents the selling price, then $0.115x$ represents royalties.

When Are We Ever Gonna Have to Use This?

The house profit margin is 6% of the cost plus royalties. This would be 0.06 (5.65 + 0.115x).

Since selling price minus royalties minus profit is equal to cost, we have the equation:

$$x - 0.115x - 0.06\,(5.65 + 0.115x) = 5.65$$

Solving for x, we get $6.82 as the selling price to the nearest cent.

Now try this one:

The manufacturing cost of a book is $7.88. The average percent of author royalties is 12.2% of the selling price. The house profit margin is 5.5% of cost plus royalties. Find the selling price.

21. **Temporary Employment Agency Clerk** (III)

The manager of a franchise temporary employment agency must pay a fee to the home office. He can pay a percentage of either the gross profit or the billable sales, whichever is less. He wishes to set up a formula for finding the point at which the two fees would be equal. This way he will automatically know which one is cheaper without computing each one for every case.

If B represents the fee rate based on billable sales and x equals the amount of sales, then the total fee would be their product, Bx.

Now let r represent the average pay rate to employees and t represent the payroll tax. The gross profit is:

$$x - (r + t)$$

If G is the fee rate based on gross profit, then the total fee in dollars would be:

$$G\,[x - (r + t)]$$

Setting the two fees equal we have:

$$Bx = G\,[x - (r + t)]$$

Find the formula for the billing rate at which the two fees are equal by solving the above equation for x.

22. Travel Agent (II)

A travel agent receives a commission on the "base" fare, before tax is added. However, in some cases the agent may only know the total fare including tax. By setting up a simple linear equation you can find the base fare and figure out the commission.

The total fare for a customer is $495.72. If this includes 8% tax, what was the base fare before tax was added? If the agent receives a 7% commission on the base fare, how much is the commission?

23. Wastewater Treatment Operator (I)

As explained in problem 52 on page 115, the amount of chlorine (A) to add to a basin is given by the formula:

$$A = 8.34FC$$

F = the flow through the basin in millions of gallons per day (MGD)

C = the concentration of chlorine in the basin in parts per million (ppm)

Use this formula to solve for the concentration in a basin after 1500 pounds of chlorine are added if the flow is 6.5 MGD.

24. Wastewater Treatment Operator (I)

The formula for detention time (the amount of time water remains in a basin) is:

$$T = \frac{V}{Q}$$

V = capacity of the basin (gallons)

Q = flow of water (MGD)

Find the capacity of a pond if the flow is 0.8 MGD and the detention time is 26 days.

Index to Occupations

Each entry lists page numbers with problem numbers in parentheses.

Accountant, 19 (1), 35 (1), 87 (1), 96 (1), 117 (1)

Accounting Systems Analyst, 25 (1)

Administrator (Shopping Mall), 25 (2), 35 (2), 75 (1)

Advertising Agent, 1 (1), 35 (3)

Airline Passenger Service Agent, 35 (4), 96 (2)

Airplane Mechanic, 1 (2, 3, 4), 9 (1, 2), 19 (2), 25 (3), 36 (5, 6), 53 (1), 68 (1), 75 (2), 87 (2)

Airplane Pilot, 1 (5), 9 (2), 19 (3), 25 (3, 4), 36 (6), 53 (1), 62 (1), 94 (3)

Air Traffic Controller, 96 (3)

Appliance Store Manager, 10 (3), 19 (4), 25 (5), 36 (7), 37 (8, 9, 10), 62 (3), 75 (3)

Appraiser (Real Estate), 10 (4), 19 (5)

Architect, 1 (6), 10 (5), 27 (14), 32 (37), 37 (11), 69 (9), 76 (4)

Attorney, 1 (7), 25 (6), 38 (12), 76 (5), 87 (3)

Auditor, 63 (4), 97 (4)

Auto Mechanic, 2 (8), 10 (6), 26 (7), 38 (13), 68 (2), 117 (2)

Biologist (Environmental), 26 (8)

Carpenter, 2 (9, 10), 10 (7), 11 (8), 38 (14), 69 (9), 76 (6, 7)

Carpet Cleaner, 11 (9), 26 (9, 10)

Cartographer, 97 (5)

Civil Engineer, 11 (10), 26 (11, 12), 30 (26), 37 (11), 77 (8, 9), 87 (4, 5, 6), 88 (7), 98 (6, 7, 8), 100 (9), 102 (15), 108 (33), 117 (3, 4), 118 (5, 6)

Computer Programmer, 20 (6), 64 (7, 8, 9)

Computer Systems Engineer, 2 (11)

Construction Supplies Counter Clerk, 27 (13), 38 (15), 68 (3, 4), 78 (10), 88 (8)

Contractor (General), 27 (14), 30 (26), 38 (15, 16), 68 (5), 69 (9), 78 (11), 88 (9, 10), 89 (15)

Controller (Hospital), 12 (11), 20 (7), 27 (15), 38 (17), 39 (18)

Data Processor, 64 (7, 8, 9)

Dietician, 2 (12), 39 (19, 20), 69 (6, 7, 8)

Drafter, 1 (6), 3 (13, 14), 27 (14), 32 (37), 69 (9)

Electrical Engineer, 64 (11), 100 (10, 11), 118 (7, 8), 119 (9)

Electrician/Electrical Inspector, 4 (15), 12 (12), 39 (21), 40 (22, 23), 101 (12, 13), 119 (10)

Engineer (see Civil, Computer Systems, Electrical, Industrial, Petroleum)

Environmental Analyst, 27 (16), 28 (17), 62 (2), 101 (14)

Farm Advisor, 28 (18, 19, 20), 69 (10), 102 (15, 16, 17), 103 (18, 19), 108 (32), 120 (11)

Fire Fighter, 12 (13), 20 (8), 63 (5), 88 (11), 103 (20), 104 (21, 22, 23)

Fire Prevention Officer, 20 (9), 40 (24), 104 (24)

Flooring Contractor, 4 (16), 68 (5), 78 (12)

Forestry Land Management Planner, 28 (21), 78 (13), 93 (1), 105 (25)

Forestry Recreation Management Officer, 21 (10), 29 (22, 23), 40 (25, 26), 78 (14)

Geologist, 41 (27), 89 (12)

Heating Contractor, 88 (10)
Highway Patrol Officer, 12 (14), 54 (2, 3),
    107 (29, 30), 108 (31)
Hydrologist, 21 (11), 42 (28), 70 (11, 12),
    79 (15), 89 (13), 120 (12)

Income Tax Specialist, 4 (17, 18), 21 (12),
    42 (29, 30, 31, 32), 43 (33), 81 (16),
    106 (26), 120 (13)
Industrial Engineer, 29 (24, 25),
    43 (34, 35), 56 (4), 65 (14), 70 (13), 81 (17),
    89 (14), 93 (2), 106 (27, 28)
Insurance Agent, 43 (36, 37), 81 (18)
Insurance Claims Supervisor, 4 (19),
    107 (29, 30), 108 (31)
Interior Decorator, 4 (20), 13 (15),
    44 (38, 39), 70 (14), 71 (15), 72 (16),
    82 (19, 20)

Landscape Architect, 30 (26), 44 (40),
    82 (21, 22, 23), 89 (15), 108 (32, 33)
Librarian, 45 (41)

Machinist, 13 (16), 21 (13), 30 (27), 45 (42),
    83 (24, 25, 26), 90 (16), 109 (34, 35, 36)
Marketing Representative (Computers),
    72 (17)
Masonry Contractor, 4 (21), 13 (17),
    45 (43), 78 (10), 83 (27), 90 (17)
Medical Lab Technician, 5 (22),
    13 (18, 19), 30 (28), 45 (44), 56 (5), 63 (6),
    65 (12), 72 (18, 19), 90 (18), 110 (37),
    121 (14)
Meteorologist, 22 (14), 45 (45), 57 (6),
    73 (20), 83 (28), 94 (3, 4)
Motorcycle Sales and Repair, 22 (15),
    30 (29, 30), 46 (46), 73 (21, 22), 91 (19)

Navigator, 67 (16), 121 (15)
Newspaper Production Worker, 5 (23)
Nurse, 5 (24, 25, 26, 27) 14 (20),
    31 (31, 32), 73 (23)

Oceanographer (Biological), 110 (38)
Optician, 22 (16)

Painter, 31 (33), 46 (47)
Painting Contractor, 84 (29)
Payroll Supervisor, 14 (21), 46 (48)
Petroleum Engineer, 14 (22), 110 (39),
    121 (16)
Pharmacist, 22 (17), 31 (34, 35), 46 (49),
    73 (24), 122 (17, 18)
Photographer, 6 (28), 31 (36), 73 (55),
    84 (30), 94 (5), 111 (40)
Plumber (County Inspector), 6 (29, 30),
    14 (23, 24), 32 (37), 46 (50), 57 (7), 73 (26),
    74 (27), 84 (31), 91 (20, 21, 22), 95 (6)
Police Officer, 14 (25), 22 (18), 46 (50),
    58 (8)
Political Campaign Manager, 6 (31),
    15 (26), 32 (38), 47 (52), 122 (19)
Printer, 6 (32), 15 (27, 28, 29), 23 (19),
    32 (39, 40, 41), 47 (53, 54), 67 (17),
    74 (28), 84 (32, 33), 92 (23)
Publishing House Order Department
    Manager, 47 (55)
Publishing House Production Manager,
    7 (33), 15 (30), 16 (31, 32, 33), 47 (56),
    48 (57), 122 (20)
Purchasing Agent, 111 (41)

Real Estate Agent, 7 (34), 17 (34), 23 (20),
    32 (42), 33 (43), 48 (58, 59, 60, 61),
    49 (62), 60 (9), 84 (34), 85 (35, 36)

Savings and Loan Counselor, 17 (35),
    33 (44, 45), 38 (16), 49 (63, 64)
Sheet Metal, Heating, and Air
    Conditioning Specialist, 17 (36, 37),
    85 (37), 86 (38, 39), 92 (24), 112 (42, 43),
    113 (44, 45), 114 (46)
Social Worker, 7 (35), 17 (38), 49 (65)
Stockbroker, 7 (36), 18 (39), 23 (21), 34 (46),
    50 (66, 67, 68), 51 (69)
Surveyor, 18 (40)

Technical Researcher, 51 (70),
    64 (7, 8, 9, 10), 65 (13), 66 (15), 86 (40),
    114 (47)
Television Repair Technician,
    115 (50, 51)

Temporary Employment Agency Clerk, 18 (41, 42), 34 (47), 61 (10), 114 (48), 115 (49), 123 (21)

Title Insurance Officer, 7 (37)

Travel Agent, 8 (38), 23 (22), 52 (71), 124 (22)

Veterinarian, 34 (48), 52 (72)

Wastewater Treatment Operator, 18 (43), 24 (23), 52 (73, 74), 86 (41), 92 (25, 26, 27), 115 (52), 116 (53), 124 (23, 24)

Welder, 8 (39), 18 (44), 52 (75)

Answers

Part 1: General Arithmetic
Fractions (pages 1–8)

1. $404 **2.** 1 1/8" **3.** 23 13/16" **4.** 3/8"
5. 2 2/5 hr or 2 hr 24 min **6.** 4 1/2"
7. $3,694,425; $1,254,167; $42,098,592
8. 1 15/64" **9.** 92 **10.** 7/8" **11.** $2900
12. Heavy: 571; Light: 286 **13.** 5 9/16"
14. 22 3/16" **15.** 108 1/4 volts **16.** 48
17. $10,160 **18. a.** 2/9 **b.** $33.33
19. $38.75 **20.** 4 sheets **21.** 18
22. 1/1024 **23.** 5 2/5" **24.** 31 **25.** 2 1/2
26. 2 2/5 **27.** 1/2 **28.** Top, right, and
left: 1 1/4"; bottom: 2 1/4" **29.** 2 1/6 ft
30. 1/4 in. per ft **31.** 99,000 **32.** Overstocked by 7/20 of a roll **33.** 1 2/3"
34. 770 acres **35.** $436.33 **36.** $3487.50
37. $516 **38.** $4032 **39.** 37 1/8"

Decimals (pages 9–18)

1. 6.51 ft **2.** 80.3—in the safe range
3. 18,240 **4.** $101,759 **5.** 153.6 lb
6. 0.0035" **7.** $1206.12 **8.** 2.80"
9. $409.03 **10.** 85.4 lb/ft **11. a.** $34.55
b. $713.08 **12.** 2.373 volts **13.** 18.1 lb
14. 3.4 hr **15.** $1793.38 **16.** 8.36 lb
17. 8125 **18.** 500.5 **19.** 18.4 microns
20. 2 **21. a.** $85.59 **b.** $389.91
22. 1.13" **23.** 5270.4 gal **24.** 336 sq ft
25. $80,144.75 **26.** $21,790 **27.** Full
carton ($81.60 vs. $96) **28.** $268.75
29. Single: $127.04; Double: $104.52
30. 240 pages **31.** $2.06 **32.** $4.50
33. a. $862.50 **b.** $0.48 **c.** $2.23 **34.** 144
months or 12 years **35.** $756 **36.** 0.0679
37. 0.3062" **38.** $2242.50 **39.** 170
40. 127.22 ft **41.** $58.13 **42.** $6.29
43. 7.6 mg/l **44.** 56.241 cu ft

Averages (pages 19–24)

1. $200 **2.** $200 **3.** 172 mph
4. $282,500 **5.** $183,050
6. $(a + b + c + d)/4$ **7.** $333.50 **8.** 257 ft
9. 6.5 **10. a.** 3.3 **b.** approx. 1270
11. 9.2 ft/sec **12.** 7% **13.** 0.7848"
14. 65.4° **15.** 12.2 per month; 146 total
16. 5 mm **17.** 235 mg **18. a.** Jones:
6.8; Martinez: 5.8; Larson: 4.3 **b.** 5.7
19. a. 5140 **b.** No **20.** $650 **21.** $6.65
22. $139.50 **23.** 0.149 or 0.15 rounded;
yes

Ratio and Proportion (pages 25–34)

1. Water—$12.51; Sewer—$4.91;
Trash—$6.58 **2.** $600 **3.** 30.8 gal
4. 145 mph **5.** 3.75:1 inventory ratio;
lasts 97 days **6.** $950 **7.** 30.17 cu in.
8. a. 28,800:1 **b.** 14,400 ft **9.** 6.4 oz
chemical, 313.6 oz water **10.** 1:2.5
11. 420 **12.** x = 35 ft; y = 44 ft **13.** 125 lb
cement, 375 lb sand, 500 lb gravel
14. 25 ft by 36.25 ft by 6.25 ft **15.** $1415.70
16. 4450 to 5480 cars per day **17.** 1.17:1
18. 22 sec **19.** 64.6 gal/acre
20. a. 58 2/3 gal/acre **b.** 2.25 mph
21. First plan: 3.88:1; Second plan:
3.44:1; first is better. **22.** 390 **23.** 125
24. 12,000 BTU/hr **25.** A,B: 1500 lb
each; C,D: 3500 lb each **26.** 8.4:1
27. 2268 rpm **28.** 88 mg/dl **29.** 12.8 oz
30. a. 3:1 **b.** 9 **c.** 75 **31.** 4 4/5 tablets
32. 12 minims **33.** 4 gal **34.** Creme A:
95.0 g; Petrolatum: 147.3 g; Univase:
237.6 g **35.** 208 1/3 mg **36.** 8 oz
37. 44 ft **38.** 303 **39.** 70.4 lb **40.** 5 1/4"
41. 24.4% (16% from first col., 8.4% from
second) **42.** $388 **43. a.** A: $56.72;

B: $127.61; C: $92.16; D: $148.88;
E: $49.63 **b.** A: $36,657; B: $82,477;
C: $59,567; D: $96,224; E: $32,075
44. J.D.: 3/8; M.S.: 9/32; S.Q.: 3/32;
S.M.: 1/4 **45.** $80,000 **46. a.** 14:1
b. $31 **47.** $276,000 **48.** 150 mg

Percent (pages 35–52)

1. Time remaining: 33.3%; Budget
remaining: 27.4% **2. a.** $1350 **b.** $1719
3. $1536.18 **4. a.** $229.11 **b.** $54.60
5. 268.8 knots **6.** 104 hp **7. a.** 19%
b. 40% **c.** 21% **d.** 156% **8. a.** Dishwasher: $486; Washing Machine:
$452.25; TV: $569.70 **b.** Dishwasher:
$413.10; Washing Machine: $384.41;
TV: $484.25 **c.** 14.75% **9.** 28.6%
10. $70,000 **11.** No (5 sq ft over)
12. 62.5% **13.** The 35% discount is
better. **14.** $276.97 **15.** $1709.02
16. $28 1st month, $98 2nd month,
$140 3rd month **17.** $1158.66
18. a. $1403.95 **b.** $1432.60 **c.** $1454.09
d. $1520.51 **19.** 1000 cal carbo., 875 cal
fat, 625 cal protein **20.** 350 g **21.** 5100
watts **22. a.** 21.16 kw **b.** yes **23.** 485–
515 ohms **24. a.** 31% **b.** 24 **25.** $660
26. a. 4689 **b.** 5516 **c.** 10,776 **d.** 18,348
total (4348 auto, 8752 trailer, 5248 tent)
27. 3.75 acre-feet **28.** 29% **29.** $1120.74
30. $288.15 **31.** $1263 **32.** $648
33. $760 **34. a.** $21,176,470
b. $23,294,117 **c.** $30,705,881 **d.** 5556 hr
35. Higher by 28% **36.** $3750
37. $782.30 **38.** $704.55 **39.** 224"
40. a. 33 1/3% **b.** 25% **c.** 11.9% **d.** 3.7%
41. a. 10.9% **b.** 64,090 **42.** 0.13%
43. Yes **44.** 472 **45.** 50% **46.** 9.6 oz
47. $165 **48.** 1st: $9000; 2nd: $7000;
3rd: $4000 **49.** 80 cc **50.** The fourth
test **51.** 1.8% **52. a.** 0.93% **b.** $8800
53. $11,523.60 **54.** 2667 **55.** $292.49
56. $25.20 **57.** $15.70 **58.** $3960
59. $4143.69 **60.** 20.3% **61.** $3055.20
62. 1st month: $250; 2nd month:
$248.75; 3rd month: $247.50 **63.** $3408

to the profit-sharing plan; $2272 to the
money purchase pension plan **64.** $300
65. a. $222 **b.** $139 **66.** Aggressive
Growth: –7.1%; Growth and Income:
–4.2%; Income: –1.9%; the Income
Fund performed best. **67. a.** The stock
b. The stock priced at $15 3/4
68. a. 10.4% **b.** 9.4% **c.** 13.3%
69. $1000 **70. b.** $16,500 **c.** $71,500
d. $2860 **e.** $10,439 Total: $156,299
71. $45.50 **72.** 2.34 lb **73.** 50.04 lb
74. 0.025% **75.** 36.72 lb

Statistical Graphing (pages 53–61)

1. a. Yes **b.** No **2. a.** 37 mph
b. 31 mph **c.** 70 mph **d.** 37 mph
3. a. 33 mph **b.** 59 mph **c.** 49 mph
4. See figure below

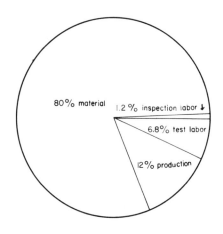

5. a. 1.8 g/dl **b.** 0.7 g/dl **6. a.** Jan.
b. Sept. **c.** 5.75 in. **7. a.** More
b. 35 GPM **c.** 60–65 GPM **d.** About 40
e. About 40 **8. a.** 1987 **b.** No; Yes (tie
with 1984) **c.** 1986 **d.** 1987
9. a. $325,000 **b.** $550,000 **c.** $440,000
d. $380,000 **10.** See figure on page 132

Miscellaneous Other Topics
(pages 62–67)

1. 48 mi **2.** 19,500,000 **3. a.** 7000
b. 3000 **c.** 17,000 **d.** 15,000 **e.** 7000

When Are We Ever Gonna Have to Use <u>This</u>?

Weekly Gross Profit per Staff Salary Dollar

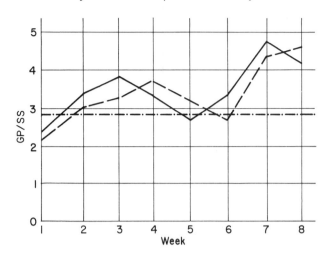

Statistical Graphing, problem 10

——— This year
— — — Last year
—·—·— Objective

4. a. $8 **b.** $12 **c.** $14 **d.** $188 **e.** $61
5. a. 275 **b.** 300 **c.** 250 **d.** 325; Yes
6. a. 5.44 **b.** 5.73 **c.** 6.00 **d.** 5.56
7. 1E70 **8.** 2734 **9.** 135 (base 8) **10.** 8
11. $1190.40 **12. a.** 5×10^6 **b.** 9.7×10^3
13. 4×10^{-10} **14.** The one-cavity die is best. (The totals were $6180 for 1 cav., $6312 for 2 cav., $6946 for 3 cav.)
15. a. 0.00009 **b.** 0.0001568 **c.** 0.0000062 **d.** 0.0000026 **e.** 0.0199822 **16.** 17.6 ft
17. −$12.15

Part 2: Practical Geometry

Measurement and Conversion (pages 68–74)

1. 55 **2.** 30/64" **3.** Yes **4.** 2 2/3 yd by 5 1/3 yd by 1/9 yd **5.** 5880 bd ft **6.** 120 g
7. 1/4 cup **8.** 400 mg **9.** 1194 ft or 1199 ft (depends on placement of siding)
10. 47.5 ml **11.** 324,000 gal
12. 2 hr 28 min 33 sec **13.** 3744 lb/sq ft

14. See figures below
a.

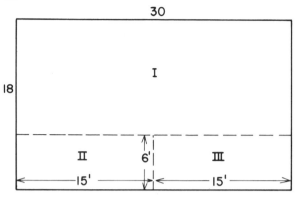

b.

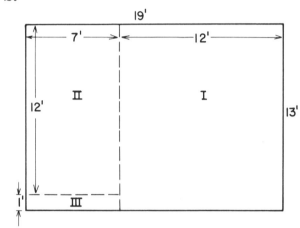

15. 8 ft **16.** 4 **17.** Yes **18.** 8.5 g
19. 3 millimoles/liter **20.** 113.3 tons
21. 1.27 cm long, 0.635 cm in diameter
22. 6.4 oz **23.** 4 minims **24.** 7 mg
25. 57.15 mm by 69.85 mm **26. a.** 3 cfh
b. 59 cfh **c.** 136 cfh **d.** 45 cfh
27. 38 ft 11 in. **28.** 2000

Area and Perimeter (pages 75–86)

1. $1717.50 (area of 1145 sq ft) **2.** 510 sq ft **3.** 7392 BTU; 3705 BTU; 6247.5 BTU; 14,040 BTU; 6831.45 BTU **4.** No; No; Yes **5.** No (19 acres) **6.** 20 ft **7.** 19 ft
8. 1.26 tons **9.** 0.210 acres **10.** 264
11. $1280 **12.** $1750 **13.** $13,114.18
14. 2252 **15. a.** A = 208 sq ft; V = 13 1/3 ft/sec; Flow = 2773 1/3 cu ft/sec

b. A = 570 sq ft; Flow = 1425 cu ft/sec
16. a. 117 sq ft **b.** 5.4%   **17.** 5399
18. $156,840   **19.** $1890   **20. a.** 42 2/3 sq yd **b.** 80 feet   **21.** $2948.83 (area of 3780.56 sq ft)   **22.** $73.58   **23.** 314
24. 5.21"   **25.** 1/2"   **26.** 7.065"   **27.** 527
28. 25.12 miles   **29.** 5 gal   **30.** No
31. 23.04"   **32.** 8818 lb   **33.** 6.6 sq in. waste per photo on the 26" by 40" sheets; 3.3 sq in. per photo on the 23" by 35" sheet
34. 72.7 acres   **35.** 31,875 sq ft
36. $328,629   **37.** 25 5/8"   **38.** 4000 sq ft
39. 5 1/3"   **40.** 200 km
41. 884.6 gpd/sq ft

Volume (pages 87–92)

1. 7666 cu ft   **2.** 41.25 cu ft   **3.** 494 gal
4. 4.12 cu yd   **5.** 28.47 cu yd   **6.** 3722.40 tons   **7.** 486   **8.** 3889 lb   **9.** 678.24 cu ft
10. No—the furnace must be rated for 12,000 cu ft   **11.** 16.6 gal   **12. a.** 200,000 acre-feet **b.** 111 years   **13.** 12,900 cu ft
14. a. 10.85 ft **b.** 8.74 ft   **15.** Yes—37 to 38 loads   **16.** 196 lb   **17.** 5.9 cu yd
18. 0.004 cu mm   **19.** 124 cc
20. a. 1228 gal **b.** about 7 ft 9 in.
21. 612 lb   **22.** No—only 4510 cu ft absorbed   **23.** 2 boxes   **24.** 64"
25. 183,110.4 gal   **26.** 53.5 ft
27. 172,800 cu ft

The Pythagorean Theorem (pages 93–95)

1. 7.2 mi   **2.** 0.117"   **3.** 102 mph
4. 14,400 ft   **5.** 43.3 mm   **6.** 51"

Part 3: Elementary Algebra
Formulas (pages 96–116)

1. 35.3%   **2. a.** 66.8 lb **b.** 213.8 lb; shipping costs: **a.** $131.93 **b.** $422.27
3. 28 nautical miles   **4.** $22,000
5. 0.35 mm   **6. a.** 100 tons **b.** 324 tons
7. 544.5 ft   **8. a.** −3.75 ft **b.** −1.67 ft
c. 362.33 ft   **9.** 0.005   **10.** 0.173 amperes
11. 48.4 foot-candles   **12.** 44.3 amperes
13. 1000 ft   **14.** 2.18 lb/hr   **15.** 302.2 cu yd

16. 58.5%   **17.** 118,200 kwh
18. 53 hp   **19.** 36 in.   **20.** 98 ft/sec
21. 328 gpm   **22.** 77 psi   **23.** 94 ft
24. Area 2 (23); Area 3 (17); Area 1 (8)
25. 18.5 to 1   **26.** 58 by the first formula; 64 by the second formula   **27.** 31.25 lb   **28.** 0.5312 in.   **29.** 52 mph   **30.** 46 mph   **31.** 0.32   **32.** 25.68 in./hr   **33.** 7%
34. 0.1139 in./in.   **35.** 0.05 hp
36. 1.5877"   **37.** 1.42×10^{-3} **38.** 1.27
39. 7.586×10^9 cu ft   **40.** 1.5   **41.** 79
42. 4100 BTU/hr   **43.** 9,352,200 BTU/mo
44. 1,032,920 BTU/mo   **45. a.** 4.67×10^6 BTU/yr **b.** 76%   **46.** 18 1/4"   **47.** 835 ft
48. 20 amperes   **49.** 6 watts
50. a. $GP = 0.97N - 1.14T$ **b.** $615.83
51. a. $10.18 **b.** The fee based on gross profit   **52.** 2001.6 lb   **53.** 14.7 days

Linear Equations (pages 117–124)

1. $1,125,000   **2.** $x + 0.06x = 14.71; $x = 13.88; tax = $0.83
3. $x + 2x + 2x + 3x = 27$; $x = 3 3/8$ cu ft; cement (x) = 3 3/8 cu ft; water $(2x)$ and aggregate $(2x)$ = 6 3/4 cu ft each; sand $(3x)$ = 10 1/8 cu ft
4. a. $y = 0.06x + 645$ **b.** $y = 873$ ft
5. $40,000 for the sidewalk; $160,000 for the pavement; $80,000 for the base material   **6. a.** 503.13 ft **b.** 1134.90 ft
7. 21,000 lumens   **8.** 60 amperes
9. 16.64 in. oz   **10. a.** $E = IR$; $R = \dfrac{E}{I}$ **b.** 220 V **c.** 0.07 ohms
11. 1.67 hr   **12. a.** 5.3% **b.** 4.5%
13. a. 20% **b.** $6600
14. $MCV = \dfrac{10\,Hct}{RC}$
15. a. $R = \dfrac{D}{T}$; $T = \dfrac{D}{R}$
b. 15 knots **c.** 3 hr 27 min   **16.** 0.45 in.
17. 22.5 cc   **18.** 56.25 g   **19.** 603 pieces
20. $9.54   **21.** $x = \dfrac{G(r+t)}{G-B}$
22. $459.00; $32.13   **23.** 27.7 ppm
24. 20.8 million gallons

Bibliography

Anthony Schools. *The Real Estate Handbook,* 1976.

Ashton, Floyd M. et al. *Weed Control Workbook.* Cooperative Extension, University of California, 1959.

Carman, Robert A. and Saunders, Hal M. *Mathematics for the Trades.* John Wiley and Sons, 1981, 1986.

Cooperative Extension, University of California. "Estimating Power Cost for Pumping Irrigation Water in the Southern California Edison Company Area." May, 1977.

Department of Transportation, Federal Aviation Administration. *Airframe and Power Plant Mechanics General Handbook.* AC 65-9. Flight Standards Service, 1970.

Garland, J. D. *National Electrical Code.* 2d ed. Prentice-Hall, 1977.

Inter-Agency Agricultural Information Task Force. "Irrigation: When and How Much."

International Association of Plumbing and Mechanical Officials. *Uniform Plumbing Code.* 1976 ed. 1975.

Marr, James C. *Grading Land for Surface Irrigation.* Circular 438. California Agricultural Experiment Station Extension Service. University of California, 1957.

McCoy, Jim. *Region 5 Constructor's and Inspector's Self-Study Courses.* U. S. Forest Service, 1969.

Pryor, Murray R. et. al. *Weed Control Handbook.* California Department of Agriculture, State of California.

Santa Barbara Police Department. *Annual Report.* 1976.

Shepperd, Fred. *Fire Service Hydraulics.* R. H. Donnelley Corp., 1967.

State Water Resources Control Board. *Operator Certification Examinations, Grades I and II.* October 25, 1975.

U. S. Forest Service. *RIM Handbook.* Forest Service Handbook 2309.11 (R-5 Supplement No. 8, August 1970. R-5 Supplement No. 14, September 1974.)